ZOROASTRIANISM AND JUDAISM

ZOROASTRIANISM AND JUDAISM

BY

GEORGE WILLIAM CARTER, Ph.D.

With an Introduction by
CHARLES GRAY SHAW, PH.D.

ARTI et VERITATI

BOSTON
RICHARD G. BADGER
THE GORHAM PRESS

MADE IN THE UNITED STATES OF AMERICA

The Gorham Press, Boston, U. S. A.

PREFACE

There is only a very meager literature on the subject about to be discussed. An attempt will be made to give an outline picture of Zoroastrianism, and then of Judaism when it came to be somewhat a fixed system in the post-exilic times. This will enable us to make the further attempt to give the leading religious, social, and moral conceptions in Zoroastrianism and Judaism, and to indicate under each heading something of the probable influence, or relation, of one system on the other. Throughout the whole discussion, the main sources of information will be the ancient literatures of the two religions. They will be referred to, or quoted, freely, in order that authority may be given for all facts stated.

It must be understood that no attempt will be made to interpret the exalted teachings of the Old Testament, as they are unfolded and revealed in the light of the New Testament. The author has firm convictions regarding the authority of the canonical Old Testament Scriptures. This treatise deals with those Scriptures in a period of time when they were incomplete and when those that were written were available only to a few.   G. W. C.

CONTENTS

ZARATHUSTRA AND THE ZEIT-GEIST

INTRODUCTION

ZARATHUSTRA AND THE ZEIT-GEIST

OUR war-consciousness, which has brought to the surface of the soul many a contradiction which time had seemed to submerge, brings Persia down to the present. Indeed, the ancient descent of Persia upon the Greek states, in accordance with the time-honored custom of warfare back and forth from east and west, is not without its analogies to the German attempt to subjugate the states which have allied themselves against the modern Xerxes. Because of the war, the contemplation of world-maps, the study of humanity's history, and the analysis of all human occupations have become objects of intensive study. The whole planet has been shaken, and the dead have risen in arms. For this reason, the study of Iranian religion and the career of Zarathustra become timely topics; the Zend-Avesta has become a war-document.

The intensity of the war has had the effect of obliterating those old lines of separation which have sought to make east east and west west; the geographical, social, and spiritual diremption of two hemispheres has been overcome; Orient and Occident blend in one supreme militarism. In the past,

Asia and Europe merely touched at the Dardanelles; in the present, there is at least a pontoon-connection between east and west. Lines of fire link London and Bagdad, military dispatches come from both Venice and Jerusalem, and the drab of khaki obscures the old-time color-contrasts of Asiatic and European modes. The Turk is in league with the Teuton, and Tokio may come to the aid of Paris. Those who come to an understanding with the times must not remain unacquainted with the biographies of Kaiser Wilhelm and Spitama Zarathustra.

The fitness of Iranian intuitions for shedding light upon the religious and political conditions of present-day Europe cannot be questioned by those who know old Persia and modern Prussia. When one consults Confucianism, he is confronted by the stolidity of Chinese ideals and the retroactive character of Mongolian motives; hence his study of the ultimate orient can amount to no more than an objective and scientific consideration of a useless and inapproachable faith. In the case of Brahmanism, there is similar defeat for him who would make practical use of remote ideals in religion. Doubtless there is much spiritual nourishment and intellectual enlightenment in Vedic beliefs, but the Hindu habit of indulging in aloofness and the tenuous nature of India's convictions conspire to make the contemplation of Vedic idealism a remote one. Their sky we cannot touch or their ideals analyze. China's impenetrable earth and India's impalpable heaven are both beyond the religious reach of the western believer. In the instance of Persia, however, there is less of this Oriental silence, even when Iranian religion is no less authentic; we ourselves are somewhat Persian in our methods of believing and doubting.

The violent wrenching of the Iranian from the Indian has in it somewhat of that separatist spirit in which the west rejoices, while the inner contradiction of good and bad, which the Persian observed in the sky and felt in the heart, is the most essential thing in European religion. Long before Greek tragedy had seen man divided against himself and ere the inner contradictions of Christian ethics had entered the heart of man, Zarathustra had felt the dismay of a soul as a house divided against itself. For this reason, Persia, which lacks the extensive majesty of Mongolian faith and the intensive dignity of Indian idealism, becomes an ally of western belief; Zarathustra reveals the Zeit-Geist.

Since the war is supposed to have sprung from the excessive egoism of the Teuton, the personality of Zarathustra becomes of special interest in the ever-intensifying days of conflict. If it is true that German giantism has developed by reason of the inflammation of the moral gland in the German brain, it is worth while inquiring to what extent Persian ideals are responsible for the painful phenomenon, especially when so many point to Nietzsche, whose

chief work of super-ethics is entitled, Thus Spake
Zarathustra. It is a question whether the egregi-
ous egoism of Prussia has been displayed with con-
sistency, or that the phenomena peculiar to its rough
manifestation have been analyzed by its moral and
military opponents; but the fact remains that the
name of Zarathustra has been linked with that of
the Kaiser, so that both Persia and Prussia are to be
studied. Lifted from his original setting, Zarathustra would feel as ill at ease in Germany as the
'Moses' of Alfred da Vigny would have felt in the
France of the 30's; but these great ones must work
for their immortal living, so that Persia's spiritual
leader must submit to resurrection in war-time. Religion is supposed to be altruistic and pacific, but
leaders of religion are often themselves noble egoistic; such was the case with Moses and Zarathustra,
with Christ and Mahomet, whose personalities present more than egoistic edge. Indeed, the whole
range of individualism in its form of the superman
is marked by the outlines of religion rather than by
politics of warfare.

Zarathustra as superman, and we have Nietzsche's word for it, tends to lend balance to an un-
certain moral situation. Those who indulge but
moderately in analysis are wont to believe that the
intrigues of diplomacy, the far-reaching plans of
politics, and the violences of war are the meat on
which the superman feeds: but those who have fol-
lowed the career of this new person cannot hide

from their eyes the fact that it is usually religion which supplies the superman with his daily allowance of heavenly manna. The superman is spiritual, rejoices in aesthetic ideals, and has a strength which lies within him. As already listed, Israel's lawgiver and Irania's guide, Galilee's seer and Arabia's prophet are typical of the character which become such a puzzle for contemporary ethics. Those who have reduced the ethics of the superman to a kind of cult have ever made use of a quasi-religious mode of reasoning; Milton and Blake, Stirner and Dostoievsky, Wagner and Ibsen found it necessary to pass by the Church when they went in search of the arch-ego. Such seers of the soul observe the superman as a sort of heaven-storming person, who either is Promethean in his fire-snatching or Zarathustrian in the noble impudence with which he buttonholes the Almighty and interrogates the skies. Thus Zarathustra questioned the supreme God, Ahura Mazda.

In the rôle of ethical educator, Zarathustra assumes an aristocratic position when he with boldness delivers to his followers the ideals which he has secured from some superior source. This at once arouses the question concerning the source and sanction of morals, and puts a sharper edge on contemporary ethical calculations. According to orthodox utilitarianism, the virtues grew up gradually and unconsciously in connection with manifest utilities and in response to democratic demands. Originally loose in the form of interests merely felt, they tightened into so many virtues of moral import. The self-styled virtue which is its own reason could have no place in the practical system of the nineteenth century, whose moral reasoning was only abetted by the evolutionary idea of progress through limitless patience and development in almost endless time. Virtue as a moral meteor which lands so mysteriously in our human field could have no place in a practical system which watched virtue grow by slow accretion and advance *pari passu* with so many felt wants of mankind. In some ways, Zarathustra tolerates such utilitarianism, and seems to contribute to the contention that virtues arise practically when there is demand for them. In this half-utilitarian manner, he speaks of 'holy wood' and 'holy meat,' while he urges that 'holiness goes on thriving' where 'the cattle go on thriving.' Such picturesque utilitarianism seeks to lay down certain general principles to the effect that 'he who sows corn sows holiness,' which special maxim seems to spring from the natural synthesis of holiness and husbandry.

But the morals of Zarathustra never abandoned their essential aristocracy, for the weight of authority which he laid upon the earth came from on high, and the pursuit of husbandry, far from being practical and self-contained, was but a special form of holiness. On the aristocratic side of the strife between sanctions, Zarathustra unconsciously offers himself as proof that ethical excellence is from above; he himself was more the child of heaven than of earth.

Morals do not spring up of themselves in the hearts of those who have interest in the virtues, but are framed above to be thrust down upon the stiff-necked and slow-of-heart. Relief from slavery among African people arises as an idea in the heart of a white man, and the slowly progressing ideals of communism among the masses was once the isolated dream of some individual. Zarathustra's Persian populace know nothing of their chief good, since contact with earth has taught them nothing; their ideals of welfare, mundane though they be, are of heavenly origin. Having observed the Good in its totality, Zarathustra finds it expedient to indulge in certain practical applications of the ideal, and thus prepares for the Persians what in a less-plausible form Nietzsche has called 'master-morality.' Zarathustra could not forego the desire to indulge in dictation, even when he points out to his people that which they might have thought out for themselves. As Moses sought the moral law at the summit of the Mount to apply it to the affairs of the desert, Zarathustra sees the Good in idea before he applies it in fact, and concludes his moral reasoning by asserting that 'holiness is the best of all good.'

In the position of revealer, Zarathustra offers practically the only rival which the seers of the Old Testament were to encounter. Passing over the extravagant claims put forth so sumptuously by Mahomet, and which came at such a late date as to suggest some imitation, the conversations between Zarathustra and Ahura Mazda cannot fail to suggest somewhat of that spiritual burden which the seers of Israel shared with Jahveh. Irania and Israel seem thus to have provided pockets for the treasures of the Most High. If the word of the Lord came to the high seers of Israel, it did not fail to pass by and swoop down over the head of Irania's chosen one, who like Cyrus seems to have been a step-son of the Almighty. But the 'revelation' which came to Zarathustra is strangely wanting in the kind of consciousness which tends to make an alleged communication authentic. Zarathustra was too confident in his humanism, and stood too erect to be a genuine prophet. In contrast with Irania's sage, who receives revelation only after he has sought it by questions, Israel never took the initiative, but on the contrary presented deaf ears and dumb lips to the enforced revelation. Moses was reluctantly recipient when the word of the Lord came to his ears, and pleaded ignorance and incapacity, voiced in the questions, 'Who am I?' and 'by what name art thou called?' The prophet could receive the word only as he beat his brow upon the earth and suffered his lips to be seared by the seraph's live coals; and when, in his almost epileptic anguish he did speak, his words sought refuge in tortuous imagery, and his spirit, lifted up, tasted the bitterness and felt the burning of truth too strong for human conception and communication. Dignity there is in the message of Zarathustra, but no divinity of distance, for the

Iranian seer spoke with confidence of such truth as he seemed to experience with Ahura Mazda. One may thus account for and accept the message of the Persian prophet by heeding it as the highest pitch in *human* register, but not the lower tones of revelation as such, even when Zarathustra may have had ears for just such music.

Dr. Carter's monograph on Iranian religion is an exceedingly painstaking attempt to square accounts with a vision whose excellence is often neglected in the midst of more perfect spiritual enlightenment. Israel will be more highly prized and better understood after Irania has been duly apprised, while Moses will mean more after the strivings of a brother sage in another land have been evaluated. Dr. Carter's method is a sure-footed one; it advances cautiously from stone to stone of textual reference. Like a Persian rug, the Zend-Avesta is made up of many a bright strand, whose patient unweaving has been the work of Dr. Carter's study. In this, there is nothing that is semi-official, since Dr. Carter has dealt authoritatively with verified reports. It is to be hoped that his book will find a place not far from our ever-growing war-library.

CHARLES GRAY SHAW.

New York University.

INTRODUCTION

"Follow you the star that lights a desert pathway,
*   yours are mine,*
Forward till you see the Highest Human Nature is
*   divine."*
                                        —TENNYSON

In the year 1700, Thomas Hyde of Oxford, the great orientalist of his time, made the first systematic attempt to restore the history of the old Persian religion and its prophet. In 1771, Auguetil Duperron of Paris published the first European translation of the *Avesta*. Little progress was made in the study of *Zend* literature until within a comparatively few years, and even now the names of those who have become eminent in the study hardly exceed half a dozen. As for a comparison between Zoroastrianism and Judaism, the most that has been done may be found in magazine articles some of which are excellent as far as they go; but they are neither exhaustive nor comprehensive. In the histories of Persia and of the Jews, general religious comparisons are made when the period of their contact is treated, but neither do these histories make any attempt or claim at exhaustive and complete treatment.

The sources of our information must therefore be the ancient literatures themselves. On the Zoroas-

17

trian side, the *Avesta* is foremost in importance. In the *Avesta,* the *Gathas* or Psalms of Zarathustra are of highest value. The *Gathas* represent Zarathustra as personally announcing a new faith. They are "the utterances of Zarathustra in the presence of the assembled church."[1] In the later literature he is spoken of as having lived in the past and often is deified, while in the *Gathas* he speaks of himself in the first person.[2] The entire Pahlavi literature is of much assistance, for it reflects through tradition the ideas of the ancient times. Herodotus and Xenophon give some facts that are valuable. On the side of Judaism, our information comes from the Bible, the Apocrypha, and Jewish writings such as the *Book of Enoch, Testaments of the Twelve Patriarchs,* and *Josephus.*

It is generally recognized that the Persians and Jews were in contact with each other, one as ruler and the other as subject, for over two hundred years, (B. C. 538-331); that during the most, if not all of this time, the faith of the Persians was Zoroastrian; that the leading teachers and authorities for the faith were Magians;[3] that there are striking similarities in some of the ideas, customs and beliefs of Zoroastrianism and Judaism. On the other hand, difficult questions are raised, for it is disputed

---

1. Article *Zoroaster,* by F. Geldner, in Ency. Britanica.
2. For exam. see *Tir Yast* I, 13, 20, 26, *Dinkard* VII. 3, 5, *Yasna* XLIII:46.
3. The Dinkard regards "the *Avesta and Zend*" as sacred writings of the Magian priests. Dk. IV, 21, 34.

whether Zarathustra is a historical character; or if he is, whether his date is early or late; whether he was born in East or West Iran; whether his birthplace was the scene of his activity. It is questioned whether Cyrus was a Zoroastrian; whether in accounting for the similiarities in religion and customs, the Persians borrowed from the Jews, or the Jews from the Persians.

In giving conclusions, I shall attempt to state and substantiate the results of personal investigation. Quotations or references will be given from the *Avesta*, Pahlavi texts, the Bible, the Apocrypha and ancient Jewish writings direct, rather than citations from the opinions of others.

Before any comparison can be made there must be an accurate knowledge of the two religions. This is absolutely essential. This may be given in a few pages, although a longer treatment would be interesting and profitable.

ZOROASTRIANISM AND JUDAISM

ZOROASTRIANISM AND JUDAISM

CHAPTER I

ZARATHUSTRA

ZARATHUSTRA was a real character. Darmesteler and Edward Meyer maintain[1] he was a mere myth. But they fail to distinguish the Zarathustra of the later literature from the Zarathustra of the *Gathas*. Zarathustra is portrayed in the *Gathas* as a man of stirring individuality, teaching, exhorting and evidently exercising a strong influence on all in his presence.[2] He is pictured as a man with strong human feelings, whose only trust is in God.[3] That he was a prophet and a reformer the growth of his religion will show.[4] The later portions of the *Avesta* represent Zarathustra in a more distant light, with somewhat of a veil of sanctification thrown around him, which serves rather to conceal than to reveal his personality. It ought not to be a matter of surprise that miraculous circumstances should be connected with him in this later literature.[5] Lapse of time has encircled other men, especially in the east, with superhuman attributes and

---

1. Darmesteler, *The Zend-Avesta,* Part I, pp. LVI. ff Edward Meyer, *"Geschichte des Allterhumus,"* v. I.
2. Ys. IX :1, XLIX :1-3.
3. Ys. XLIII :8, XLVI :1.
4. For the work of the prophet and reformer, see pgs. 25 and 26.
5. Yt. XIII :93, XVII :19, Vd. XIX :6, Dk. VII.

deeds.

The date of Zarathustra was fixed by some classical writers at 6,000 B. C.[6] This was perhaps due to the Greeks' misunderstanding statements of the Persians regarding Zarathustra's millenium in the great world period of 12,000 years. Other ancient writings connected Zarathustra with the mythological Semiramis and Ninus, with Nimrod and Abraham.[7] The direct Zoroastrian tradition[8] is clear and strong in placing Zarathustra's date between 250 and 300 years before the time of Alexander, which would be in the late seventh century or the earlier half of the sixth century, and before the Achaemenian dynasty. This view which is also in harmony with the most recent scholarship, seems the most reasonable to adopt.[9]

The familiar form of the prophet's name, Zoroaster is from the Latin Zoroastres, which in turn is modelled after the Greek *Zwsoá's Tsns*. In the Pahlavi texts the usual form is Zaratust, of which modern Persian has a variety of expressions. All of these are variations of the *Avestan* Zarathustra. It is a prosaic name and perhaps means old camel. The family designation was Spitâma.

In Zarathustrian literature, there is general unanimity in fixing Zarathustra's birthplace in West

6. Plato, *Alciabiades* I :122.
7. Eusebius, "*Chronicon,*" I :43, IV :35.
8. Bund. XXXIV :1-9, *Ardai Viraf* I :1-5, Dk. VII. 7 :6, *Zad-Sparam* XXXIII :11-12.
9. For discussion of Zarathustra's date see, West, *Pahlavi Texts*, Part V, pp. 27-47 and Jackson, *Zoroaster*, appendix II.

Iran, either in Adarbaijan or in Media.[10] He seems to have been "without honor in his own country," and to have wandered in different places engaged in labors.[11] Many details of Zarathustra's early life and of his later experiences are given in Pahlavi literature.[12] He is the son of Powmshaspa and Dughedha. His lineage and ancestry are traced in detail. His life is a series of marvels. Omens and prodigies attend his birth. Sorcerers and enchanters endeavor to destroy the young child, but all their efforts are fruitless. Necromancy, sorcery and the black art are constantly resorted to, all of which Zarathustra defies. He even rebukes his father for yielding to such influence.

At about twenty, he withdraws and gives himself to thought and meditation. This is the period of preparation common to all great teachers. At the age of thirty when he is by the river Avetak the revelation comes.[13] It is parallel to the vision of Daniel.[14] The archangel Vohumanah (good thought), the Gabriel of the faith, appears and leads Zarathustra to a conference with Ahura Mazda, which is the first of seven[15] visions with hallowed communings, which he enjoys during the next ten years. After the first vision, he preaches reform to the heretical priesthood and people of the land, but

10.   Bund. XX :32, XXIV :15, Vd. XIX :4, 11, I :16, Ys. XIX :18.
11.   Ys. XLVI :1, Yt. XIX :66.
12.   Dk. VII :2-7, Dk. V :2-3, Zad-Spm. XIII-XXIV.
13.   Dk. VII :3, 51, Z.-Spm. XXI :1-27.
14.   Dan. X :4-12.
15.   Spm. XXII :1-13, Ys. XLIII :5-16.

with no success.

In disappointment he wanders for years, and his first convert was not won till after ten years. He was his own cousin, Maidhyo-Mah.[16] At the bidding of Ahura Mazda, Zarathustra now goes to the court of Vishtaspa. Here after discouragements for two years, by a miracle finally being performed on the king's favorite horse, the king is won for the faith.[17] Vishtaspa becomes a great helper in propagating the religion through Iran and beyond.[18] The pictures given in the *Gathas* of the court scenes are striking. The voice of the reformer curses the daevas and the ungodly, and promises to the righteous the rewards of heaven.[19] Zarathustra speaks not only as a reformer, but as a prophet of Ahura Mazda he announces a new doctrine to man.[20]

The religion spread rapidly after the conversion of Vishtaspa. The holy wars against the Hyaoman leader Arejat-Aspa, who twice invaded Iran formed the great events of the last ten years of Zarathustra's life.[21] The victory for the faith was complete and the religion became finally established. It was during the second invasion that Zarathustra probably perished, at the age of seventy-seven, (perhaps in

16. Ys. LI :19, Yt. XIII :95, Bd. XXXII :2, Spm. XXIII: 1-2.
17. Dk. VII :4, 70-85, Ys. LI :16.
18. Dk. V :2-12. S-g Vig. X :64-70, Yt. XIII :99-110, Ys. XXVI: 9, Vsp. XVI :2.
19. Ys. XLVI :14, XLIX :9, XXVIII :7-8, XLIV :9.
20. Ys. XXXII :1-2, XLIV :1, 11, XLV :5, L :1.
21. Dk. VIII :11 :4, VII :4, 77-87, 88-90, Yz. §§ 58-85, ShN. Mohl IV, 330-340. Vishtaspa prays for divine aid in battle. Yt. V :109, IX :30-31, X1X :87.

B. C. 563). Pahlavi texts always speak of a murderer.[22]

After the death of Zarathustra the religion continued to spread.[23] Had it not been for Marathon, Salamis, and Plataea the worship of Ahura Mazda might have extended into Europe. The greatest teacher who rose was Saena,[24] who lived in the first and second centuries after Zarathustra. It was his disciples, Alexander overthrew when he came in his world conquest. He brought ruin by the sword and burned the books of the *Avesta*. It was a dark period for the religion. But with the national power broken, the sacred books burned, Zoroastrianism lived on, and in the third century A. D., it rose to supremacy again through the Sassanian empire. (226-651 A. D.). Sects like the Manichaean arose, heresies like that of Mazdak came in, but the religion held its old glory till in the seventh century, it was almost blotted out by the armies of Mohammed.

Only about ten thousand true followers of Zarathustra are to be found still in the old Persian home. Others had preferred exile to conversion to Islam, and took refuge in India, where they found safety, peace and freedom to worship Ormazd. The Parsees of Bombay, their true descendants, number about ninety thousand. They are a flourishing community and faithful to the ancient creed.

22. Dk. VII:5, 1, V:3, 2. Z-spm. XXIII:9, Sad. Dar. IX:5.
23. Dk. VII:6:12, 7:6, VIII:14, 10, Zspm XXIII:11, Yt. 13:97.
24. For the names of other successors of Zarathustra see Zspm. XXIII:11ff. Pahlavi Texts.

CHAPTER II

JUDAISM

A DETAILED treatment of Judaism would it-self furnish an instructive theme for a book. To give within a few pages a right estimate of Judaism is not an easy task, and to do so in order to indicate its relation to a foreign influence is still more difficult. Many facts concerning persons and events must be assumed as known and accepted in order that the leading features that pertain to the life and religion of the Jews before, during, and after the exile, may be brought prominently before the mind.

Judaism was a unique politico-religious organism. Its fundamental principles came to be an acknowledgment of the one God, Yahveh, and of the Torah in which Yahveh revealed Himself. It began with the reform of Josiah. That reform indeed practically had failed in Judah, but during the exile the teachings proclaimed by the pre-exilic prophets prevailed. Before Josiah's time society was rotten to the core.[1] The prophets of the eighth century, Amos,[2] Hosea,[3] Isaiah,[4] Micah,[5] had rebuked the people for their sins and called for righteousness to

1. Zeph. I:5-6, 8-9, III:1-4, Jer. II:5, 12, 22-27, 34.
2. Aos. II:4-5, VII.
3. Hos. VI:4-11, XII:2, 6.
4. Isa. VII:6-9, XXII:8-12.
5. Micah I:5, III:5-6.

the Holy One of Israel. As a result there was a reformation under Hezekiah, but under Manasseh and
Amon the masses returned to their old idols.[6] Nev-
ertheless the spirit of reform was in the air when
in 639 B. C. the little Josiah came to the throne. By
rebuke and appeal Zephaniah[7] and Jeremiah[8] and
Nahum[9] moved the people to the first steps of reform again. The finding of the book of the law
within the temple[10] gave character to the reformation.[11] Jeremiah, whose heart and soul were in the
work of reform, welcomed the covenant,[12] and the
people publicly assembled by the king, pledged themselves to keep it.[13] With the reformation of Josiah
begins the rule of written law. This was decidedly
a great advance. The written requirements were
superior to the earlier ceremonial forms, and also
gave a stability to the worship of Yahveh it had not
possessed before. This written law a part of our
present Book of Deuteronomy (v-xxvi, xxviii) is sat-
urated throughout with a broad, prophetic spirit. It
is the book of Love in the Old Testament.[14] The
detailed laws are the means whereby this love is to
find expression. It set apart the followers of Jeho-

6. II Kings XXI :73.
7. Zeph. I :12, I :8, II :1-3.
8. Jer. V, VII :1-7.
9. Nahum. I :15, II :1-2.
10. II. Ki. XXII :1.
11. Ki. XXIII :1-28.
12. Jer. XI :2-6.
13. II. Ki. XXIII :3, III Chron. XXXIV :33-35.
14. Deut. VI :5, VIII :2-6, X :12, XI, 1, 13, 22, XIII :3, XX :4.

vah as a holy people[15] High places were swept away
and the temple at Jerusalem was exalted and made
the only place of sacrifice.[16] It started literary activity which left its impress on all later Hebrew literature.[17] Under the kings succeeding Josiah there
was reaction and apostasy.[18] During the closing
years of Judah's existence, Jeremiah stood almost
alone,[19] her last and greatest prophet. He declares
the overthrow of the short rule of Egypt (609-605)
by Nebuchadnezzar,[20] which was the beginning of the
end for Judah. Earnest and pleading appeals for
reform were of no avail.[21] The people were un-
righteous and rebellious, and their doom foretold
came upon them. "Jerusalem became heaps, and
the mountain of the house as the high places of the
forest."[22]

The few Jews who remained in Judah were in
pitiable circumstances.[23] Not so were those in exile.
For the most part their bondage was not an oppres-
sive one.[24] Many lived in their own homes and some
obtained wealth. But the true Israelites could never

15.   Deut. VII :6, XIV :2, 21, XXVI :1, 9, XXVIII :9.
16.   Deut. XII :2-5, XXVI :2, I Ki. VIII :29, Psa. LXXVIII :68.
17.   The literary products of this period may be indicated in
part by Deut., Jer., Judges, Sam., Kings, Zeph. and some of the
Psa. and Prov.
18.   Jer. X :21, XI :10, 13-17, XVIII :17.
19.   Jer. VII :8, VIII :8, 11, XI :18-23.
20.   Jer. XLVI.
21.   Jer. XVII :5, 7, XIX, XX, XXXIV, XXXVIII.
22.   Micah III :12.
23.   Lam. III :45-53, V :1-18, Jer. XL :11-12.
24.   Jer XXIX :5-7, Isa XLI :6-7, XLIV : 10.20, Baruch VI.

be reconciled to Babylon.[25] In exile they maintained their religion separately. This is undoubtedly the chief reason they did not dissolve and perish in captivity. The harm Babylonia had done in the years before the exile in exciting to idolatry, it undid in the years of banishment.

With the accession of Cyrus and the rule of Persia, came the permission to return to their cherished land.[26] The undertaking was difficult. Years passed before those who returned succeeded in rebuilding the temple. It was not dedicated till 516 B. C.,[27] more than a hundred years after the reform of Josiah, and it was not till 445 B. C. that the walls of Jerusalem were rebuilt.[28] Ezra, Haggai, Zechariah, and Nehemiah were prominent figures in shaping the life of the community, especially Ezra and Nehemiah. Following the rededication of the walls there was social and religious reform,[29] and of greatest importance the adoption, by a great assembly of the people, of the Covenant, the priestly code.[30] The reformation under Josiah had been by a royal decree and its influence still continued in Judah. The priestly reformation was democratic. By a popular vote, the people accepted the new law

25. Ezek. IV:12-15, Hos. IX:3, Psa. CXXXVII:1-5, Isa. XLII:22.
26. Ezra VI:3-5, Ezra I:1-4.
27. Ezra III:8, Hag. II:3-9, Ezra VI:1-15, Zech, VIII:9-15.
28. Neh. II:7-8, VI:15-16.
29. Ezra X, Neh. VI:17-19.
30. Neh. IX, X. The code though not then completed, was in the main in Exo. XXV-XXXI, XXXIV:29 to end, and the books of Leviticus and Numbers.

and bound themselves by an oath to walk in God's law.[31]   The new code centred the life of the true Israel about the sanctuary, and hereafter more and more Jerusalem was to be the holiest place upon earth.   The code united all faithful Jews whether in Palestine or in other lands, encircling them with a high wall of separation. For they all now had one law, one worship, and one temple. Judaism no longer meant a nationality but a religious conviction.

Another element in the growth of Judaism, which from this time exerted a strong influence, was the Samaritan schism.   Josiah's reform had left a lasting impression upon the Samaritan people,[32] but many heathen ideas survived.[33] The challenge[34] they gave the returning Judeans to prove themselves the people of Yahveh was finally met by the declaration that Sanballat and his followers should "have no portion, nor right, nor memorial in Jerusalem."[35] When the Jewish community solemnly bound itself by the priestly code the Samaritans were forever excluded from the Jerusalem temple. The two communities continued to live in bitter rivalry and jealousy, both laying claim to the name and privilege of the ancient Israelitish nation.   The Judeans were fired by the Samaritans to a passionate devotion to their law and temple, and much of the intolerance

31. Neh. X :28-29.
32. II Kings, XXIII :15-20.
33. Isa. LXV :11, LXVI :3, Neh. IV :4-5.
34. Josephus Antiquilies, XI :2 and 8.
35. Neh. II :20.

which disfigured later Judaism was the result of the conflicts with the worshippers on Gerizim.

Thus Judaism came to be a fixed system. The inner forces and external influences that shaped the system may be more or less distinctly traced, and need be indicated only briefly. A strong inner force was the literature of the period, helping to give character to its life and thought.[36] There was the priestly aristocracy whose functions and power from the time of the adoption of the priestly code were ever widening. Of greater influence still were the new religious teachers, the scribes. Their power increased as that of the prophets waned. They became the dominant intellectual leaders of Judaism. They edited and expanded the Law. They made its practical applications. Their place of instruction was the synagogue, which was a recognized institution shortly after the time of Ezra. It became as democratic as the temple was exclusive. There resulted a devotion to the Law, to know and to keep which was a glad privilege.[37] Emphasis was placed upon the individual instead of the family or tribe. This was first brought out by Jeremiah[38] and Ezekiel.[39] There developed in Judaism a self-centered, intellectual, strong moral-religious life illustrated by lofty ex-

36. In addition to the pre-exilic literature mentioned above (pg. 15 note 1) there was Lam. Ezek., Job, Deutero., Isa., Hag., Zech., Mal, the Priest Code, some of the Psalms, the Wisdom literature, and the apocryphal writings.
37. Psalm XIX:7-11, LXXXIV:1-2, CXIX.
38. Jer. XXXI:30-34.
39. Ezek. XXXIII:1-20.

amples of probity and piety.

Among the external influences several may be named. Before the exile the Hebrews were tempted by foreign courts into idolatry, and into political and social extravagances. Yet by contact with foreign powers, they gained a conception of a broader world than they had known before. This, too, gave them a sense of the power of organization. The Babylonian exile represented a fundamental transformation in the political, social and religious life of the people. It proved that the Jewish people could maintain their racial separateness without king or political organization. The energies of the leaders were turned from politics to ritual and religion. Idolatry was forever stamped out, and the religion became pure monotheism.

The religion and rule of Persia was one of the external influences. It will be treated later. On the return from the exile, the influences of their heathen neighbors led to the erection of that high wall of separation which not only excluded the Gentiles, but kept the Jews faithful to their race and religion. They could not have political ambitions as in earlier days, for they were a subject people, but they were free to devote all their time and energies to religion.

In the Greek period, Greek worldiness, philosophy, radicalism, were resisted by Jewish legalism, simplicity, and conservatism. The contact of such contrary forces proved rich in results for the world. But it brought into bolder relief the antagonistic

features of Judaism. The Jews could refuse to be
Grecized. The furnace of affliction in which Judaism was long cast only intensified the loyalty and devotion of its followers. They evidenced for centuries a fearless passion for their religion.

The conditions among the Jews operating against
the giving or receiving of foreign influences may for
the most part be reduced to their exclusiveness. The
exile was a period of rapid change. Previously,
they often had been following the ways of other nations, and at the same time boasting of their own in-
violability. After the exile, they were glad to accept
the message of prophet, priest, or scribe in their
eagerness to obtain reconciliation with Jehovah.
Their ruling desire was to regain their lost national
and individual purity. The great prophet of the
exile declared that because of their peculiar relation
to Jehovah they had a high mission to fulfill among
the nations.[40] But his ideal was too exalted for
those of his time to appreciate. The presence of
their enemies, the Babylonians, Persians, and the
heathen in Judah, united the Jews by an indissolu-
ble bond. Persecutions only intensified their loyalty
to their adopted creed. The horror of being absorbed into the great heathen world led them to
become exclusive of everything foreign. When they
thought of their neighbors it was to pray for their
destruction.) There was an opportunity for the ad-

40. Isa.. LXII:1-2, LV:1-5, LIII, LXVI:1-2.

mission of proselytes, but there was little or no proselyting.[41]   In the Greek period the broad tolerance of the book of Jonah found little illustration. There was the same race-pride, rigid ceremonialism, and religious passion.   Yet there were striking inconsistencies which indicate that Judaism absorbed, perhaps unconsciously, foreign ideas and beliefs.

In the sixth century B. C., the Aryans came to the front in influence and power, and the Hebrews came into contact with them as subjects.   It was during this period, and the years immediately following, that the Hebrews became known as Jews, that they were changed from being a nation into a politico-religious theocracy, that their leaders instead of being statesmen became priests and scribes, that the people placing themselves in bondage to a rigid law became religious in their ambitions, instead of secular or political.   There was an over-emphasis of ceremonial righteousness, there was constantly a spirit of exclusiveness.   Yet in the writings of the time there was also emphasis given to moral righteousness,[42] to the expectation of a useful future for Israel as Yahveh's servant,[43] to a world-wide conception of Yahveh's love and care.[44]   There was a higher conception of worship than at any earlier time.   The synagogue with its Torah and prayer did much to

41. Deut. XXIII:7-8, Lev. XVII:8-10, 13, Num. IX:14, Exo. XII:48.
42. Later Psalm and Deutero.-Isa.
43. Deutero.-Isa.
44. Deuero.-Isa., Joel, Jonah.

create a more spiritual idea of worship. There was a truer recognition of the sovereignty of holiness by which alone they could hope for national perfection. However hollow their religion may have been, this recognition was an omen of good.

The Jews came into direct touch with Persia in the Babylonian exile and for more than two hundred years afterward. Cyrus, the Persian king, "the righteous one, the Shepherd of the Lord, the anointed of God,"[45] gave orders that the temple at Jerusalem be rebuilt and that the Jews be returned from captivity to their own city.[46] Darius, the worshipper of Ormazd, favored the rebuilding of the temple and commanded that the decree of Cyrus be carried into effect.[47] Judea became a Persian province and remained so till the time of Alexander. There are probably references to the ancient faith of Persia in Ezekiel and Deutero-Isaiah.[48] The Wise men who came from the East to worship Christ, were Magi, followers of the ancient creed of Persia, and it is actually stated in the Apocryphal New Testament that they came in accordance with a prophecy of Zarathustra.[49]

The chief characteristics of the Zoroastrian religion in brief are: the philosophic tenet which recog-

45. Isa. XLI:2, XLIV:28, XLV:1-3, 13.
46. II. Chron. XXXVI:22-23, Ezra I:1-17, III:7, IV:3, I Esdras II:1-7.
48. Ezra VI:1-15, I Esdras III:42-57.
48. Ezek. VIII:16, Isa. XLV:7, 12.
49. Infancy III:1 cf. Mt. II:1-2.

nizes the constant warfare that rages between the good principle Ahura Mazda, or Ormazd, ('Ορομάσδης) and the evil spirit, Angro Mainyu, Ahrmian, ('Αρείμάνιος), and their respective kingdoms. The duration of this conflict is limited, at the end of the world good will triumph, and evil be annihilated; a general resurrection of the dead will take place and the new life begin. There is also in the religion an elaborate system of angels and demons, a distinct cosmology and cosmogony, a pronounced doctrine of eschatology, and a high code of ethics. There are also elements of nature worship, a deification of sun, moon and stars, a religious veneration for fire, earth, and water, and a scrupulous awe in exercising care to preserve these elements from defilement. These nature features seem to point back to earlier times. In addition there is a rigid dogmatism that inculcates the necessity of preserving the purity of the body, the care of useful animals, the practice of agriculture, and the observance of a strictly defined ritual.

To bring Judaism and Zoroastrianism more clearly into view, the beliefs wherein they agree may be summarized briefly. Each was proclaimed by a prophet. Each worshipped one God. Each believed in an evil power. Each forbade images. Each laid emphasis on a moral act. Each was intolerant toward other systems. Each developed priestly cults, and emphasized ceremonial cleanness. Each had something like a synagogue worship. Belief in angels and demons and in the future life were ideas common to both.

Surely with so many points of agreement here at once were influences that would tend to unify them. During all these years in which Judaism was gradually assuming form the most intelligent and active members of the Jewish race were brought into continued contact with the dominant peoples of the age.[50] Since in other respects their habits were changed by the new environment, it would have been strange indeed if their religion had been unaffected. The Babylonians were too gross in their idolatry to develop Jewish religious conceptions. But the Jews were attracted by the faith that had so many articles in accord with their own teachings.

The policy of the Persians towards the Jews also would render the Jews favorably disposed toward their rulers.[51] There is evidence, too, that during the Persian period the Jewish community received many foreigners into its midst.[52] The influences which tended to keep the two religions apart were, that the Hebrews were so little known, so little in contact with other peoples, and their priesthood so exclusive, that it is not likely they would

50. "Mordecai the Jew was next unto king Ahasuerus, and great among the Jews, and accepted of the multitude of his brethren; seeking the good of his people." Esther X:3; also Esther VII:8, VIII:7-17, Dan. VI:1-3, 14, 28, VIII:3.

51. Isa. XLIV:28, XLV:1-4, II Chron. XXXVI:22-23, Ezra I:1-4, II Macca. I:18-24, 31-35, Ezra VI:1-15.

52. Zech VIII:22-23, Isa. LVI:3-8, "Many of the people of the land became Jews." Esther VIII:17

exert any strong influence upon Persian ideas. The Persians being rulers would have made this influence less likely. On the other hand, the Jewish horror of heathen nations together with their devotion to the covenant, erected that high wall of separation which isolated Judaism during more than four centuries. Further, during a large part of the Persian period, the attitude of the satraps toward the Palestinian Jews would not dispose the latter consciously to imitate. Those in the Dispersion would not consciously have adopted Persian ideas when their hearts said, "How shall we sing the Lord's song in a strange land."[53] No important belief of Judaism was adopted outright from the Iranian faith, but without foreign influence some of the leading beliefs would not have been grasped and so fully developed, as they appear to have been from this time. To trace the resemblances between the two religions, and to indicate something of the probable influence of the one upon the other will occupy the remainder of this volume.

53. Psa. CXXXVII :4.

CHAPTER III

THE IDEA OF DEITY

IT is natural that the idea of deity should claim first attention. Everywhere in Iranian scriptures the supremacy of Ahura Mazda is recognized. So characteristic is this supremacy that Mazdaism is the name sometimes used for the religion. Ahura Mazda is invoked as "the creator, the radiant and glorious, the greatest and the best, the most beautiful, the most firm, the wisest, and the one of all whose body[1] is the most perfect, who attains His ends the most infallibly, . . . who sends His joy-creating grace afar; who made us and has fashioned us, and who has nourished and protected us, who is the most bounteous spirit."[2] There are passages in the Avesta that indicate the divine unity,[3] yet the unity is incomplete.[4] At times Ahura Mazda seems to be but one of the seven Immortals,[5] (Amesha Spentas) who govern the universe. His power is limited, too, by the presence of Angro-Mainyu,[6] else the Persian reasoned he would not permit the existence of evil.

1. Ahura was not conceived of as having a body proper. The stars are elsewhere described poetically as his body.
2. Ys. I :1.
3. Ys. XXXI :7-8.
4. Ys. XXX :4-5, Yt. XIII :1, Ys. LVII :17.
5. Sirozah II :1, Dk. IX :27, and many Yts.
6. Ys. XXXI :12, Bund I :8, 13-20, Vend. I :3-20, Yt. XV :3-4, Yt. V :17-18, XIX :46.

This means that his omnipotence is in doubt, though it is sometimes implied and even asserted.[7] The spitituality of Ahura Mazda is a high conception often expressed. He is the bountiful and holy spirit.[8] This ideal of spirit is implied in other attributes. He is Lord-Wisdom which may be said to be the chief characteristic of Ahura Mazda. In a chapter of the Avestan ritual, which was recited daily, Ahura Mazda says of himself, "My sixth name is Understanding. My seventh is the Intelligent One. My eighth name is Knowledge. My ninth is Endowed with knowledge. My twentieth name is Mazda (the All-knowing One). I am the Wise One; my name is the Wisest of the Wise."[9] He is omniscient[10] He is everywhere represented as creating with intelligence,[11] while his antagonist Angro-Mainyu creates with ignorance. Holiness and goodness are attributes of Ahura Mazda.[12] His relation to men is represented in the *Gathas* as personal,[13] though it may be the personal relation was confined to the prophet Zarathustra. He is the friend and helper of men, and deeply interested in their welfare. He is declared to satisfy their "spir-

7. Ys. XLIV :3-5, 7, Sk-G. Vig. III :5-6, Yt. I :12.
8. Ys. I :1, XXVIII :1, XLIII :2, XLIV :2-7, XLVII :1-2, Shl-Sh. XV :2-3.
9. Yt. I :7, 8, 15.
10. Ys. XXXI :13, XXIX :4, XLV :4, Yt. I :8, 12, 13-14, Vd. XIX :20, Bund I :2.
11. Ys. XXXI :7, XLIV :3-5, Yt. I :7-8.
12. Ys. XXVIII :7, 10, II :2, Yt. I :7, 12.
13. Ys. XXXI :14-18, XLIV, XLVI :1-12, XXVIII :12.

it's need."[14] Anthropomorphic ideas are more rare in the *Gathas* than in the Bible. Those that occur must be regarded as symbolical or a result of poetic license. Ahura Mazda was not to be thought of as having a human body.[15] To Zarathustra he was a spiritual, incomprehensible being, as Yahveh was to the poets and prophets of the Jews. Because Ahura Mazda is said to sustain a fatherly relation to some of the Amesha Spentas, does not detract from the purity and ideality of his conception.[16] It is as though he were affirmed to be the father of all goodness Out of some such a conception perhaps came the idea of the fatherhood of Yahveh which later reached a high development.

On the great Behistun rock near the old Median boundary, three hundred feet from the base of the rock, is the inscription of Darius which reads: "The great Ahura Mazda which is the greatest of the gods has made Darius king. He has delivered the kingdom to him. Through the grace of Ahura Mazda is Darius king. This saith Darius the king. This land of Persia which Ahura Mazda gave me, and which is beautiful, rich in herds, rich in men population, through the grace of Ahura Mazda fears no foe. May Ahura Mazda grant me aid, together with the clan gods,[17] and may Ahura Mazda protect

14. Ys. XLVI:2, XXXI:21, XLIII:1-3, XXVIII:11.
15. Ys. LVIII:8, XXXVI:6, are later than the Gathas, and symbolical on their face.
16. Ys. XXXI:8, XLV:4, XLVII:2, Yt. XVII:16.
17. The clan gods are parallel to the Amesha Spentas and may perhaps mean them. See L. H. Mills in The New World for 1895, p. 47.

this country from hostile hosts, from evil developments and from the plotting lie, and this favor I
beseech of Ahura Mazda with the clan gods." In
the inscription at Nakhs-i-Rustem Darius is represented as saying, "A great God is Ahura Mazda,
who made this earth and yon heaven, who made man
and provided the happiness of home for him, who
made Darius king, the alone ruler of many. . . .
I am king through the gracious will of Ahura Mazda. O man think no evil. The command of Ahura
Mazda is this: think nothing evil, leave not the right
way, sin not." Other inscriptions, those of Xerxes
and Artaxerxes, those at Alwand and Persepolis, are
as striking in their praises of Ahura Mazda. The
words *vasna Auramazdâha,* (by the gracious will of
Ahura Mazda) occur again and again throughout
the inscriptions. The inscriptions as well as the literature indicate the high idea of deity held by the
Persians.[18] The kings mentioned in these inscriptions ruled during the Persian period of Jewish
history.

Before going further, it is well to inquire at this
point what was the idea of God held in earlier times?
No fully satisfactory answer can be given. A stage
of primitive animism with all its spiritism, fetichism
and ancestor-worship is assumed by students of religion. An advancing step would be natural religion, with the personification of natural phenom-

18. Cuneiform Inscriptions, R. A. S. J. Vol. X.

ena, and merging into polytheism. Traces of these stages may be found surviving in the *Avesta*. Herodotus says[19] that from early times the Persian people worshipped the sun, moon, earth, fire, water and stars. These were all Indo-Iranian divinities. In the inscription of Darius quoted above, he appeals not only to Ahura Mazda but also to the clan-gods. The clan was a recognized institution in Iran, and under the protection of the religion. Zarathustra would only have to exalt Ahura Mazda and ignore the lesser divinities, and the step from polytheism to monotheism would be taken. If this was the step taken by Zarathustra it certainly was not taken immediately by the people. The new faith could not have sprung up suddenly. There must have been an antecedent stage. There may have been a decadent faith. The *Pahlavi Dinkard* and portions of the *Avesta* imply that Zarathustra had to contend with superstition, sorcery and devil worship. Zarathustra declares he longs to purify the religion,[20] and he will be a guide to all who will turn from their evil ways.[21] Mithra, "the lord of wide pastures," the Yazatas of light and truth, has been thought by W. Geiger to come from a pre-Zoroastrian nature worship.[22] The Iranian Mazdaism, as it was before the reform of Zarathustra and the *Gathas,* was probably the re-

19. Herod I:131.
20. Ys. XLIV:9.
21. Ys. XXXI:2, LI:13, LIII:2, XLIII:3.
22. Geiger, Civilization of Eastern Iranians, V, I, Introduction VI. See also Yt. X:1, 7, 10, 12, 24, 48, etc., Ys. I:3, II:3.

ligion of Cyrus, so much as he had; though that reform was undoubtedly earlier than his reign. This would easily allow him to recognize Merodach, or Yahveh. He was a polytheist or whatever suited his immediate purpose. The Magi were in Media and Babylonia perhaps in the seventh century. They are mentioned in Jeremiah[23] and Herodotus.[24] Their religion was non-Aryan, but its presence should be recognized at least. The idea of deity in pre-Zoroastrian times must have been in accord with a nature worship and an existing polytheism. Zarathustra was a prophet of a new faith.

The God Zarathustra proclaimed represented a very high and pure conception. His throne was in the heavens, in the abode of endless light.[25] Around him stood the angels. These were the Amesha Spentas.[26] The evil spirit alone disputed his authority. If an angel seemed for a moment to be his peer, he was not eclipsed. Ahura Mazda was "the great God, the greatest of the gods," as he is called in the Achaemenian inscriptions. He was the being of infinite moral light, truth and purity. He was truth, and holiness, the All-knowing One. The loftiness of the conception was not paralleled anywhere save in the sacred writings of the Jews. The dignity, the spirituality, the privity of Ahura Mazda is well worthy of comparison here.

23. Jer. XXXIX:3, 13,
24. Herod I:101, 108.
25. Ys. XXVIII:5.
26. Ys. XXX:9, XXXI:4.

In the earlier days, Yahveh was to Israel what Chemosh was to Ammon.[27]   He was the tribal God.   He was the storm God.   He was not the only existing God, but the exclusive God of Israel.   This conception continued for centuries.   The Hebrews could serve only Yahveh, to serve another God would be for them a wrong.   This was henotheism.   National misfortunes were regarded as tokens of Yahveh's displeasure.[28]   Success was a proof of divine favor.   If therefore, the Hebrews were the one people of Yahveh, His glory was dependent on their national prosperity.   He would surely vindicate Himself.[29]   Yahveh was served by ceremony and offering, and little emphasis was put upon social and private morality.   Idolatry continually menaced and marred the faith.[30]   While Yahveh continued the tribal God, the conception of Him became broader and nobler in the minds of many of the nation's leaders.   Amos emphasized that Yahveh was righteous, and hinted He was the God of the universe.   Hosea announced that Yahveh was just because his love was supreme.   But these prophets were far in advance of their time.   Isaiah, too, exalted the holiness of Yahveh as a moral perfection.   He was the

27. Judges XI:24. On the origin of the cult the period of animism, ancestral worship and the growth of religious ideas. See the histories of Grätz, Kuenen, Renan, Wellhausen.

28. Amos IV:6-13.

29. Amos V:18.

30. I Sam. XXVI:19, II Sam. XXIV:6, I Ki. XVIII:18-21ff, XXII:43, II Ki. XXI:6, XXIII:7, 10, Isa. II:8, 20, Micah I:6-9, Jer. II:11, 26-28.

"Holy One of Israel." The prophets of the eighth century do not expressly declare, though their teachings may imply it, that Yahveh is God alone. It is in the age of Deuteronomy and of the later writers that Yahveh's sole Godhead is emphasized. This conception as well as the movement toward universalism was aided by contact with the great empires. The exile purified to a large degree the popular half-heathen idea of Yahveh. The people were made to feel their dependence on Yahveh who rules supreme in the universe. From this time there developed the truth that Yahveh rules in human affairs, which is strongly expressed in Job, Deuteronomy, Isaiah, Zechariah, and some of the Psalms.[31] Yahveh was no longer a tribal God, but the universal God and Ruler, and His house was to be "called a house of prayer for all peoples." Yahveh was supreme above all other gods.[32] The post-exilic writers emphasize the attributes of Yahveh. The wisdom,[33] omnipotence,[34] holiness,[35] justice,[36] love,[37] are frequently

31. Zech. II:11, Job. XXXVIII ff, Isa. LVI:3-8, LXVI:1-2, Psa. LXVII, LXXXVI:9, CII:15-22, II Esdras XVI:76, Jud. IX:11.
32. Deut. XXXII:39, II Esdras XIII:15, Baruch IV.
33. Job. XII:13, XXVIII:24-27, Psa. CIV:24, CXXXIX:1-3, Dan. II:20, Mal. III:6, Prov. III:19, Isa. XLII:9, XL:13, 14, 28, Wisd. VII:24-30 et al.
34. Isa. XLVI:10, Psa. CXV:3, Dan. IV:35, II Esdras VIII: 20-24, VI:1-6.
35. Psa. CXI:9, XCIX:9, Isa. XLIII:15, XLIX:7, LVII:15, Lev. XI:44, XXI:8.
36. Job. XXXIV:12, XXXVII:23, Eccle. III:17, XII:14, Psa. XCIV:2, Exo. XXXIV:5-7, II Esdras VII:44.
37. Deut. XXIII:5, Isa. XLIII:1, XLIX:15, LXIII:7, Dan. IX:9, II Esdras V:36-40, VII:62-70, VIII:47.

mentioned. The personal[38] and spiritual[39] relation
between Yahveh and His people, between Yahveh
and the individual worshipper are definitely and
strongly represented. There was a gradual giving
up of old anthropomorphisms and a growth in the
idea of Yahveh as pure spirit.

We are not to suppose that Zarathustra borrowed
the conception of Yahveh directly or indirectly. The
cult of Ahura Mazda has a national stamp in spite
of resemblances to the worship of Yahveh. Be-
sides we have placed the reform of Zarathustra
and the *Gathas,* earlier than the period of Persian
rule over the Jews. And it is in the *Gathas* that
we find the highest and most spiritual conceptions
of Ahura Mazda. In later times these conceptions
degenerated, rather than were elevated by contact with other people. On the other hand the Hebrew idea of Yahveh immediately after the exile
took on a richer and broader content. How shall we
explain it? In part by foreign influence. That influence was certainly not Babylonian polytheism,
save as it operated negatively. The intimacy between the Jews and the Persians, when we remember
the exclusiveness of Jewish religious feeling, can be
explained only by recognizing the similarity between
the two creeds. The Jews would have been attracted by the lofty conception of Ahura Mazda. In ac-

38. Isa. LXII:5, Psa. CIII:13, Job. XIII:4, Wisd. V:5, XVI:
26, Eccles. XXIII:1, Wisd. XVI:26, II Esdras I:28, 88, II:2.
39. Isa. XLVIII:16-17, Job. XXXIII:4, II Esdras XVI:62,
Psa. XXXIV:20, LI:10, Wisd. I:2, II Esdras I:37, VII:62-68.

counting for some of the attributes, the personal and spiritual qualities which Yahveh had from this time, it seems probably that for them the Jews were indebted to the worshippers of Ahura Mazda; that through Zoroastrian influence the Jews were led to grasp attributes and qualities of Yahveh which previously had been latent. To the new ideas of Yahveh the Jewish people gave a loftier and purer, and more human meaning than their foreign neighbors had done. Worshippers of Ahura Mazda did not cenceive such truly personal and spiritual relations, as devout Jewish writers of the time declared existed between Yahveh and His followers.[40] Yahveh was supreme, the one Lord in whom they trusted, the God of heaven.[41] They were never tempted to surrender Him. In one striking particular He always had been above the Iranian deity. He was omnipotent. Ahura Mazda was constantly assailed by the power of evil. In a future millenium he would gain the victory and be supreme, but he was not now. The Jewish faith had no such device to explain the presence of evil. Yahveh was supreme over all. It is not unlikely that the author of Deutero-Isaiah may have had the Zoroastrian faith in mind, when he represented Yahveh as saying, in an address to Cyrus, "I am the Lord, and there is none else; beside me

40. See page 41, notes 5 and 6; also Deut. IV :29, VI :5, Psa. XXXVIII :1, XL :11, CXLV :8, 9.

41. Perhaps the term "God of heaven," may have been Persian, any way it is most frequently used in this period. Ezra VI :9, VII :12, Psa. CXXXVI :2, Neh. I :4, II :4, Dan. II :18.

there is no God. I am the Lord and there is none else. I form the light, and create darkness; I make peace and create evil; I am the Lord, that doeth all these things."[42]

If every religion have some note more dominating than the rest, dualism is the prominent factor in the religion of ancient Persia. The dualism does not exclude other elements, for there is a strongly marked monotheistic tendency as we have seen. The dualism was an attempt to solve the problem of evil. Ahura Mazda or Ormazd makes what is good in the world, Angro-Mainyu or Ahrinan mars it. The good god dwells in endless light, the evil deity in infinite darkness. The home of the blessed is in the south, of the damned in the north. The most striking passages of the dualistic scheme of the world are found in the *Gathas, Vendidad* and the *Bundahishu,* and are easily found in other Pahlavi literature.[43] In the "Iranian sermon on the mount,"[44] the antithesis of the two primordial spirits is definitely given, and their contrasted natures pointed out. In the *Gathas* Ahura Mazda is God with Spenta Mainyu as his "Holy Spirit;" the Druj, "Lie, Falsehood," is the devil, with Angro Mainyu as his "Evil spirit." In the opening of the Vendidad the action and counteraction of Ahura Mazda and of Angro Mainyu are

---

42. Isa. XLV:5-7.

43. Ys. XXX:3-5, XXXI:12, XXXII:3-6, 9, XLIV:15-16, LI: 9-10, Vend. I, III:7-11, XIX:1-14, XXII, Bund. I, III, VI, XXVIII.

44. Ys. XXX:3-5.

described. The dualism dominates the cosmogony, the cultus, the entire view of the moral order of the world. Not only does Angro Mainyu spoil by his counter-creations all the good creations of Ahura Mazda, but he brings death into the world, seduces the first pair to sin, brings forth noxious animals and plants, and surrounds man by evil spirits. The dualism is clear; whether it was pre-Zoroastrian may not be answered so readily. Dualism may be claimed to be earlier Iranian or even Indo-Iranian in origin, but in its characteristic Persian form, in its moral and ethical aspect we may believe it originated with Zarathustra. Zarathustra's dualism is a monotheistic dualism, and an optimistic dualism, since Ahura Mazda will be finally victorious and good will triumph. It has been argued that because no dualism is recognized in the inscriptions of the Achaemenian kings, that therefore they were not Zoroastrians or did not believe in dualism. But the reasoning is based upon *e silentia* grounds. The absence of dualistic elements in those inscriptions is not more marked than the non-mention of the devil in a royal edict or presidential proclamation of our time. It is also to be noted that *Drauga*, (Falsehood, Lie), is almost as much a satanic personage in the Achaemenian inscriptions as is Druj in the *Gathas*.

The modern Parsees claim that in *Spenta Mainyu* of the *Gathas* there is a phase of Ahura Mazda's being which is the antithesis of Angro Mainyu; and they conceive of Ahura Mazda as comprising within himself the two spirits, the good and the evil. There is no question but that Spenta Mainyu, or Holy Spirit, is often conceived in the *Gatha* as an emanation from Ahura Mazda. In such cases it becomes personified; it sometimes plays the role of intermediary, especially in creative activity. As Spenta Mainyu is of the same nature and substance with Ahura Mazda, the subtle relation between the two is almost as hard to define as that between the Holy Spirit and the Father in the New Testament. The natural drift of the system, however, was to dualism. The monotheistic tendencies of its theology could not withstand the dualism of its philosophy. But the theology made the dualism optimistic as has been indicated.

Only a few sentences need be given to dualism in Judaism. The subject will be involved later in our discussion of angels and demons. In the earlier days Yahveh, though only the tribal God was sole and supreme in the tribe. Yahveh was the author of every phenomenon, good or evil. After the exile the Jews awoke to a realization of the spiritual, antagonistic powers of evil, as they had not known them before. It is not unlikely that the author of Deutero-Isaiah may be rebuking Persian dualism in the words, quoted above,[45] "I form the light and create darkness," etc. An instance in the development

45. Page 50.

of these ideas may be indicated in the books of Sam
uel and Chronicles, the former compiled several cen
turies before the latter. In Samuel,[46] Yahveh is
angry with Israel and moves David to number them.
In Chronicles,[47] Satan "provoked David to number
Israel." { The conception of Satan in Zechariah,[48]
Psalms[49] and Job[50] we probably may attribute to
foreign influence. } He is represented as planning
man's ruin, causing ills and disasters, and even exercising a sort of government. But the Jewish dualism is different from the Persian in this, that Yahveh
is never eclipsed or held in subjection even for a
time. He is always supreme. The work of Yahveh's creation, as it is told in the early allegorical
parables of Genesis, may be marred by the presence
of evil,[51] but neither here nor elsewhere is Yahveh's
power limited. He is always stronger than Satan
and all the powers of evil. Yahveh, too, existed before the evil came into being. The Jewish dualism
was not complete.

46. II Sam. XXIV:1.
47. I Chron. XXI:1.
48. Zech. III:1-2.
49. Psa. CIX:6.
50. Job. I:6-8, 12, II:1-7. See also II Esdras III:21, Baruch
IV:7, 35.
51. Gen. III:1-15. The origin of the particular form under
which the adversary appeared, need not be discussed, as it does
not bear directly upon our theme. See Keunen, Renan, etc.

CHAPTER IV

THE HOST OF HEAVEN

IN the scriptures of Zarathustra's faith, goodness,
light and heaven are portrayed as waging inces-
sant warfare against evil, darkness and hell. The
host of heaven and the celestial hierarchy are pictured in clear colors. The host of hell and the in-
fernal bands are less distinct, but they are not too
shadowy and dim to admit of being outlined. The
armies of the two kingdoms are almost marshalled
in warlike array.

The Greeks with their anthropomorphic ideas of
the pantheon of heaven were impressed by the ideal
and spiritual character of the Iranian divinities.[1]
They noted, too, the absence of images among the
Persians. Some images there were and Ahura Mazda is sculptured on the Behistun rock in Achaemenian times, but this meant little more than our
own carvings of angels, or representatives of deity
in earlier Christian art.

The supreme ruler of the heavenly host, of the
kingdom of good, of light and of truth was Ahura
Mazda, the Lord God of Iran. The spirituality
and loftiness of the conception of Ahura Mazda has
been already indicated. He is the all-wise god, omniscient, benign, and bounteous, righteous and im-

---

1. Herod I :131, III :29, 37, VIII :109.

mutable, undeceiving and undeceived, a guardian and protector, the father and creator of all good things. He, on his throne in the heavens, in the realm of eternal light, is surrounded by a company of ministering angels who do his bidding. These are the archangels, "Beneficent" (Spenta) "Immortals" (Amesha), or Immortal Holy Ones. They are six in number, and together with Ahura Mazda they constitute a seven-fold group or celestial council. Their names are personifications of abstract concepts or virtues, Vohn-Mano, Good Thought, Asha-Vahista, Righteousness, Khshathra-vairya Material Sovereignty, Spenta-Annaiti, Wisdom in Piety, Haurvatat, Health, and Ameretat, Life or Immortality.[2] The separate names of these abstractions are frequently found in the *Gathas*,[3] while a list of their names in the order given is in many places elsewhere.[4] In the metrical *Gathas* the group title does not seem to be found, but is often met with in other Avestan writings.[5] The adjectives *Vohn, Vahista, Vairya,* and *Spenta* which are the titles of the first four respectively are the standing epithets, inseparable from each. No adjective seems to be assigned to *Haurvatat* or *Ameretat*. In later literature the *Amesha Spenta* are augmented by other

2. Yt. II:1-3, Siroz. I:1-7, Yt. XIX:16-17, XIII:83-84, Dk. VII:2, 18, Zad-Spm XXI:13, VII:3:17, 51.

3. Ys. XXVII:3-5, XLV:10, XLVII:1.

4. Ys. I:2, Yt. I:24-25, Bund. I:25-26.

5. Ys. XLII:6, XXXIX:3, Vsp. IX:4, XI:12, Ys. IV:4, XXIV:9, LVIII:5, Yt. XIII:82.

names included as archangels, but this is not Zoroastrian.

Ahura Mazda is the father and creator of the Amesha Spenta.[6] He brought them forth to aid him in his work. Their creative and organizing activity is part of their character as agents of Ormazd.[7] By preference he acts through their ministering hands[8] The Amesha Spenta receive special worship in the ritual, and are said to descend to the oblation upon paths of light.[9] In paradise they sit upon thrones of gold.[10] Each has a specific character and sphere.[11] Vohn-Mano is the personification of Ahura Mazda's good spirit and divine wisdom. He is Ormazd's first creation and the chief promoter of the kingdom. He welcomes the souls of the blessed,[12] and is the archangel who leads Zarathustra to Ahura Mazda.[13] The name is associated with peace as opposed to discord.[14] In the material world, Vohn Manah has especial charge of useful animals.[15] Asha Vahista is the personification of right representing divine law and moral order in the world. To live according to Asha was the Zoroastrian ideal.[16] All fires are especially under the genius

6. Yt. I :25, XIX :18, II :1-3.
7. Yt. XIX :18-19, LVIII :5.
8. Ys. XXVIII :7.
9. Yt. III :1, XIII :84, XIX :17.
10. Vend. XIX :32.
11. Sh-l-Sh. XXII :1-7.
12. Vd. XIX :31-32.
13. Ys. XXVIII :3.
14. Yt. II :1, 6.
15. Ys. XXXI :10.
16. Ys. XXXI :2.

of Asha Vahista.[17] Khshathra personifies Ahura
Mazda's might, majesty, sovereignty, representing
the triumph of regal power. He presides over the
metals which stand as his sign and symbol.[18] Spenta
Armaiti, a feminine being, daughter of Ahura Mazda and heaven, is the personification of religious
harmony and piety. She presides over the earth
which is a symbol of her bounteousness.[19] Hauo-
vatat and Ameretat are two feminine archangels
always mentioned together. The first is a personification of complete health, perfection, the
other of immortality. They are the promised
reward of the blessed after death in paradise.[20]
Their charge is the water and the plants, and is mentioned as early as the *Gathas*.[21] Each of the Immortal Holy ones has a special month assigned to his
honor,[22] each has a special day as a holy day, and
each has a particular flower as an appropriate em-
blem,[23] Along with Ahura Mazda they are worshipped and propitiated.[24] Everywhere in the Zoroastrian system, the existence of the Amesha Spenta
is a characteristic feature, and it is probable the doctrine originated with the Prophet himself.

The Yazatas, "adorable beings" stand third in

17. Yt. XVII :20.
18. Yt. X :125.
19. Vd. II :10-11, 14-15, 18-19, Ys. XVI :10.
20. Ys. XXXIV :11, XLIV :17, XLV :5, 7, 10, XLVII :1, Yt.
I :25, Siroz. II :6-7.
21. Ys. LI :7.
22. Bund. XXV :20.
23. Bund. XXVII :24.
24. Yt. XIX :14-20, Vsp. XIX :1-2, Sh-l-Sh. XV :4-31.

rank, and serve like the Amesha Spenta still further
to carry out the will of the divine Lord, Ahura Mazda.   Their number theoretically is legion, and they
are spoken of as rising up by hundreds and thou-
sands.[25]   In practice, however, the only prominent
Yazatas seem to be those to whom a day in the
month is assigned, as a holy day, or to whom a special season or form of ritual worship is consecrated.
The days for Ahura Mazda and the six Amsha-
spands should be deducted.   There are spiritual,
heavenly, and material, earthly Yazatas recognized.   At the head of the heavenly division stands
Ahura Mazda, who is called "a Yazatas and the
greatest of the Yazatas."[26]   The chief of the earthly Yazatas is Zarathustra.   Grouped together, the
Yazatas are the guardians of the sun, moon, stars,
and heaven, of the earth, air, fire, and water; or
they are personifications of abstract ideas, like Victory, Truth, Uprightness, Peace, Power and kindred
conceptions.[27]   Some of these Yazatas receive much
attention, and have very important functions, especially Fire, Water, Sun, Mithra.

The Fravashis are a mighty army of spirits, belief in which is quite characteristic of the faith of

25. Yt. VI:1.

26. Yt. XVII:16.

27. An enumeration of the principal Yazatas is to be found
in Ys. XVI:3-16. Most of our details are from the Yasts. For
Fire Yazatas see Ys. XVII:1-11, Water Yt. V, Sun Yt. VI, Moon
Yt. VII, Star Yt. VIII, animal creation Yt. IX, Mithra Yt. X,
Sravsha Yt. XI, Rashme Yt. XII, Victory Yt. XIV. For other
Yazatas see Yts. XV, XVI, XVII, XVIII.

Iran. The recognition of these genii probably dates from very early times. They help Ahura Mazda and also mankind by warning against evil, keeping guard, and promoting all that is useful and advantageous. Special worship is paid to these good genii. The first month of the year is sacred to their name, and a festival of several days is held in their honor. The thirteenth yast is devoted to their praise.

Just as each principal Yazatas is associated with some Amesha Spenta, so there are a number of lesser divine beings associated with the Yazatas themselves. They are coadjutors, auxiliaries of the angels. Most of these spiritual creations are embodiments of virtues or personifications of noble traits. Fabulous or mythological creatures are also recognized, but the fact need only be mentioned. Belief in them, perhaps, is tolerated because they are survivals from an older stage of the religion.

A sufficient outline has been given of the host of heaven, so that, in order to our purpose, only a little need be said of the opposing powers of darkness. Zoroastrianism attempted the solution of the problem of evil by maintaining from the beginning, a dualism of forces, one good and beneficent, the other evil and destructive. On the one hand is Ahura Mazda supported in his work by the archangels and angels, on the other hand is Angro Mainyu surrounded by a body of evil spirits and demons. Angro Mainyu is the highest, the prince among the evil spirits. He is the counterpart of Ahura Mazda, bringing forth only evil, while the latter brings forth only good. He existed along with Ahura Mazda as is expressed clearly in the *Gathas*:

"The two spirits who first of all existed, the twins
 proclaimed to me of themselves.
The good and the bad in thoughts, words, and works,
And of those two the intelligent selected the right
 one, but fools did not so.
When the two spirits came first together, in order to
 create
Life and death, and (to order) how the world should
 be at the end,
Then the most evil one appeared on the side of the
 impious, but the best spirit appeared on that
 of the pious."[28]

The same antagonism is expressed in the following:

"I will announce the two spirits at the beginning of
 the world:
Of them spake the blissful also unto the destructive:
Neither our thoughts, nor our commands, nor our
 intelligence,
Nor our belief, nor our speeches, nor our deeds,
Nor our doctrines nor our souls correspond."[29]

Whoever causes goodness, at the same time injures the evil spirit. No wonder, then, Angro Mainyu was distressed at the birth of Zarathustra

28. Ys. XXX:3-4.
29. Ys. XLV:2.

who brought men to the true faith and to piety. His distress is painful: "Born, alas, is the holy Zarathustra in the house of Porushaspa. How can we contrive his destruction? He is a blow against the Daivas, he withstands the Daivas, he is an opponent of the Drujas; the worshippers of the demons shall fall down headlong."[30]

As Ahura Mazda surrounded by the Amesha Spenta and Yazatas is in the kingdom of light, so Angro Mainyu surrounded by the demons is in the kingdom of night and darkness. To the Amesha Spenta the group of six arch-demons are opposed as enemies in the same way as their chief and prince is opposed to Ahura Mazda.[31] They form the immediate associates, to some extent the court of Angro Mainyu. The special foe against Vohu-Mano is Akomano,[32] the evil mind; against Asha-Vahista is Andra or Indra, perhaps an old nature god who in the new religion is banished to the company of demons; against Khshathra is Saru, (the tyrant); against Spenta Armaiti, Naoghatya is named, who is sometimes identified with, sometimes distinguished from Taromat, (arrogance). Over against Haurvatat and Ameretat are Taru and Zarika, evil hunger and evil thirst. The arch fiends aim to destroy the work and influence of the good spirits. There are many other evil spirits "co-operating and confederate with

30. Vd. XIX:46. See also Dk. VII:4, 36, 57-62, Vd. XIX: 1-4, Zspm XIV:8.
31. Yt. XIX:96, Bund. XXX:29, I:27, III:2.
32. Bund. XXX:29, Yt. XIX:96, Bund. XXVIII:7-14.

them."[33] "Demons, too, who are furies are in great multitude. They are demons of ruin, pain, and grɔwing old, producers of vexation and vile, revivers of grief, the progeny of gloom, and vileness, who are many, very numerous, and very notorious."[34] Individual demons need not be further mentioned. Enough has been said to indicate the belief in a great body of evil spirits, some of which appear more prominent and powerful than others.

We have then to inquire how the host of heaven, and the host of hell, in Zoroastrianism, are related to parallel conceptions in Judaism. Much has been written concerning Jewish angels and demons, and only the ideas that bear upon our discussion will be touched.

In the earlier Hebrew days the angel is represented as a being charged with divine authority. It is such a being that appears to Hagar,[35] to Joshua,[36] and to Manoah.[37] It is a distinct angel or messenger, for Yahveh could not be called His own messenger. The fact that evil spirits are said to be sent from Yahveh, perhaps may be due to the nature of their work rather than to the character of the spirits.[38] But there are many traces of magic, and necromancy is a well defined art.[39] The angels stand as simple ministers or messengers of Yahveh, sometimes ap-

33. Bund. XXVIII :12, 14-46.
34. Bund. XXVIII :37-38.
35. Gen. XVI :7-13.
36. Josh. V :13, 15.
37. Judg. XIII :15-21.
38. Judg. IX :23, I Sam. XVI :14-23.
39. I Sam. XVI :23, II Ki. III :15, I Sam. XXVIII :3-20, Isa. VIII :19, XXIX :4.

pearing in bodily shape. In pre-exilic times they belong to popular rather than to prophetic religion. They occur in the earlier books almost exclusviely in the so-called folk-lore stories while the prophets are nearly silent concerning them.[40] After the exile, however, angels spring into prominence and are a distinctive feature of the religion. This prominence is seen in the writings of Ezekiel and Zechariah. The conceptions of these writers is far surpassed by later Judaism. For then we discover the highly developed system and hierarchy of angels, which is represented in Daniel and Enoch, and in still later times is everywhere recognized. It became in time a vast and intricate system colored by prurient imagination, superstition, and foreign elements, and is described in the most hyperbolic language. In the time in which the Jews were in touch with the Persian religion, not only a complete system of angels was developed, but we find the abstract idea of angels and spirits, and names and numbers for spirits all of which is parallel to Zoroastrian conceptions. Yahveh is represented as surrounded by a great multitude of angels who do His bidding.[41] Among these there are archangels, sometimes they are called Watchers and Holy Ones,[42] sometimes they are distinctly re-

40. Angels are mentioned 15 times in Genesis, 10 times in the Balaam story, 10 times in the story of Manoah, 22 times in all of Judges, 14 times in Samuel and Kings. See Weber, "System der pal. Theologie," §§ 34, 35, 48, 54.

41. Psa. LXVIII:17, CIII:20, CIV:4, CXLVIII:2, II Esdras II:42, 46, II Macca. X:29, Enoch X:1-15, VI:3, XVI:66.

42. Dan. IV:13, 17, 23, cf. I Tim. V:21, Enoch XII:2, 3, XIV: 1, XV:18.

ferred to as the seven holy angels. "I am Raphael, one of the seven holy angels, which present the prayers of the saints, and go in before the glory of the Holy One."[43] As Ahura Mazda was recognized as one of the Amesha Spenta, and together they were called the seven Immortal or Holy Ones, it seems probable that the developed Jewish conception which came into prominence at this time had a Persian source. This is implied further in the number seven often occurring in sacred symbolisms.[44] It is after Persian influence that we find names given to the archangels, Gabriel,[45] Michael,[46] Uhiel,[47] Raphael. The Book of Enoch names the whole seven archangels.[48] Long lists of names of angels occur in Enoch, and in other later literature.[49] The names of the Biblical angels are Hebrew, which we would expect on the supposition that the Jews took general conceptions from the Persians and molded them in accordance with their own habits of mind. In the development of these ideas for which Judaism was so largely indebted to Persia, we find, however, the name of one Persian daeva, Asmodcus.[50] The Fravashis in the Zoroastrian faith are at once the souls of the deceased, and the protecting spirits of

43.   Tobit XII:15, also Enoch XX, cf. Rev. V:5, VIII:2.
44.   Ezek. XL:22, 26, XLIII:25-26, XLIV:26, XLV:22, 23, 25, Zek. III:9, IV:2, 10, Dan. IV:16, 23, IX:25, cf. Rev. V:6.
45.   Dan. VIII:16, IX:21, cf. Jude 9. Rev. XII:7. Luke I:19-26. 4. Dan. X:13, 21, XII:1, 5-7.
46.   II Esdras IV:1, and 6. Job III:17, V:4, XII:15, VIII:2.
47.   Enoch XX:1-7.
48.   Enoch XX.
49.   Bereshith R. Talmud, 48, 56.
50.   Tobit III:8.

the living, created before their birth and surviving
after their death.   They appear in Judaism as
guardian angels,[51] and perhaps are the good angels
of the second Book of Maccabees.[52]   The idea of
angels as spirits, and of spirit as representing the
inward being of God is a Jewish conception at this
time.[53]   The personifications of wisdom in Job[54] and
Proverbs,[55] and still more strongly in later literature,[56] suggest the personifications of the Amesha
Spenta in the *Gathas*.   The Jews in such speculations
had more to learn than they could teach.   Later,
Philo of Alexandria blended ideas from the Old
Testament and Greek philosophy which he thought
equally inspired.   He framed his conception of the
δυνάμεις, powers, logic, angels, which were agents between God and the world.   The Logos is their sum
collectively, through whom God deals with the world
and with men.   The Logos is wisdom, creator, medi-
ator, interpreting God to men, and being the God
of imperfect men.   Darmesteter, holding to a late
origin of the *Gathas,* advanced the theory that the
doctrine of the Amesha Spenta was due to Neo
Platonic influences, that Vohn Mano was a reflection
of θειος Λογος of Philo, and that the other Amesha

51.   Psa. XCI:11, XXXIV:7, Zech. IV:1, Dan. X:13, 20-21,
cf., Matt. XVIII:10.
52.   II Macca. XI:6, XV:23, also Enoch LXX:4, 9-12, Tobit
V:21, Acts XII:15.
53.   Isa. XL, VIII:16, LXIII:9-10, Job. XXVI:13, Psa. LI:12,
Dan. IV:8.
54.   Job XXVIII:12-23.
55.   Prov. VIII:22-35.
56.   Ecclus. I:4, Wisd. IX:9-11, VII:25-29, et al.

Spenta were parallel to Philo's Δυνάμεις, powers.[57]
The manner in which Vohn Mano is spoken of in
the *Avesta* is often strikingly parallel to expressions
used of the Logos by Neo-Platonists. But some of
the names of the Amesha Spenta were of common
occurrence by the end of the Achaemenian period,
and the doctrine of archangels existed and was accepted at that time. It seems more likely that Philo
gathering ideas and elements from every source may
have borrowed also from the rich Zoroastrian creed.

Much that has been said concerning angels applies
to the development of the idea of demons. The
early traces of magic and necromancy already have
been spoken of.[58] The conception of a personal
spirit of evil who is hostile to Yahveh was a growth.
In the days of Ahab a scene is presented from the
councils of Yahveh in which a spirit is commissioned
to be a lying spirit.[59] In the vision of Zechariah,
there appears an angel to accuse Joshua, who bears
for the first time the title, "Satan," the "Adversary."[60]
These are trusted officials; so is Satan in the prologue
to the Book of Job,[61] but his attitude has become
more antagonistic. The development is seen in the
passage in which the chronicler makes Satan instead
of the Lord move David to number Israel.[62] Satan
develops into a distinct personality, an enemy of

57. Jewish Quar. Review, Vol. VII, pp. 173-195.
58. Page 63.
59. I Ki. XXII:19-23.
60. Zech. III:1-2.
61. Job. I:6-12, II:1-7.
62. Page 48, II Sam. XXIV:1, compared with I Chron.
XXI:1.

Yahveh and all good, and he is surrounded by a
hierarchy of evil spirits who do his will. The number of demons is legion, and the names of many are
given.[63] The Testament of the Twelve Patriarchs
mentions two groups of seven evil spirits, as if in
contrast to the seven archangels.[64] Belief in the
power of demons is an accepted faith.[65] Satan is
the head and ruler of the evil spirits.[66] The beginning of all evil is ascribed to these evil angels.[67]
They bring only ruin and death to men.[68] The parallel between Satan and Ahriman or Angro-Mainyu
is obvious. But the Jews conceived of Satan as a
fallen creature. His existence and the partial triumph of the powers of evil does not impugn the
sovereignty of Yahvah. The archdemon is far from
being equal to Him. The sovereignty of Ahura
Mazda is, however, continually assailed by Angro
Mainyu. In the Persian faith the sense of evil is so
strong as to give rise to practically an evil deity. In
the Jewish faith, the conception of Yahveh is so
strong as to keep the evil powers in practical sub-
ordination to Him. But for the development of a
system of demons, with names and evil functions
such as the Jews came to hold, they were probably
borrowers from the Persian religion.

63. Enoch VII:9.
64. XV:8, LVIII:1-22. Testa. Reuben.
65. Josephus, Anc. Ant. VIII:2, 5.
66. Enoch LIII:3, VIII, IX, X.
67. Enoch LXIX, Wisd. II:23-24, Ecclus XXI:27.
68. Baruch IV:7, 35, Job. VI:7, 14, VIII:8.

CHAPTER V

NATURALISTIC TRAITS

IN the Zoroastrian doctrine, the universe is a product of the goodness of Ormazd. He called it into existence. It is marred only by the malicious attacks and deeds of Angro Mainyu, or Aharman, the Bundahis name. The earth is the scene of the conflict between these two beings, the rulers of good and evil. Man is the centre of the universe, and his soul is at stake as the prize for which they contend. Two primeval spirits are assumed to exist at the beginning.[1] The good spirit, Ahura Mazda, dwells above in eternal light; the evil spirit lurks in eternal darkness. They meet and struggle in the realm of Time, which Ahura Mazda has carved out as a special period for the history of the world.

This time forms an aeon of twelve thousand years, divided into four periods of three thousand years each.[2] Each of these is presided over by a sign of the Zodiac Perhaps in this Zodiacal system there may be Babylonian influences. The first three thousand years is the period of spiritual creation. Ahura Mazda at the outset, through his omniscience, knows of the existence of Aharman. He therefore produces the whole of his creation in a spiritual state, and

1. Ys. XXX:3, XLV:2.
2. Bund. I.

the creatures so produced, remain in a transcendental form for the first three thousand years of time. This primordial spiritual creation by Ahura Mazda is exemplified in the *Fravashis* and alluded to in the *Avesta*. Aharman, ignorant but malicious, arises from the darkness and is confounded at seeing the light. Ahura Mazda proposes to the evil spirit a period of conflict for nine thousand years, because he knows that at the end the evil spirit will be undone. On terms being accepted, he at once routs Aharman, who flees back to darkness and remains three thousand years in confusion. The weapon Ahura Mazda uses is the sacred prayer Ahura Vairya. This holy word resembles the part the Logos plays in Neo-Platonic ideas of creation.[3]

In the second three thousand years Ahura Mazda brings into tangible shape the creation which had hitherto existed only in spiritual form. At the same time Aharman produces demons and fiends which aid him in his warfare against heaven. The order of Ahura Mazda's material creation after the Amesha Spenta and the spirits, is, first, the sky; second, water; third, earth; fourth, plants; fifth, animals; sixth, mankind. The Fravashis, or celestial prototypes, also aid in this creation as they do in the management of the world. It is by deliberate choice that the guardian spirits of men, Fravashis, elect to be born into the world, in order to aid in the overthrow of Aharman and to win joys eternal.[4]

3. Bund. I.
4. Bund. II:10, DK. VIII:7:11-13.

In the third three thousand years, Aharman having recovered from his confusion, and encouraged by the demoness Geh (like Milton's conception of sin), heeds his fiendish hosts and springs like a snake[5] through the sky down to the earth. The vault of heaven is shattered, earth is in distress, blight, corruption, disease, and noxious creatures are everywhere found.[6] He assaults water, earth, plants, and the fire; pollutes them, and slays the primeval bull, (Gos), and the primal man (Gayomard). The heavenly angels finally gain the victory and hurl the fiends to hell beneath the earth, while they build a rampart around the sky to protect it against the adversary. But as the primordial bull and man pass away, they become the progenitors of all animal life and mankind. The remainder of these three thousand years is the history of the race and of the kingdoms of earth till the coming of Zaratust, (Zarathustra).[7]

Zaratust and his sons, Ausheta and Aushetarmah, together with the coming of Saoshyant fill the Fourth period of three thousand years. At the close of this period, Ahura Mazda will triumph over Aharman, and good will be supreme.[8]

In the late traditions, and still more in the older literature, it is plain to see, that the pious mind of

5. Bund. III:1-7. With Gen:1-24.
6. Bund. III:1-17, Zad-Spun. II.
7. Bund. III:18, IV:5, XXIV, XXVII, X, XIV, Yt. XIII:86-87.
8. Bund. XXX, XXXII:5-9.

the old Iranian, beheld in all the phenomena and wonders of nature the ever-working power of the Deity. "This I ask Thee, O Ahura! tell me aright: who by generation was the first father of the Righteous order within the world? Who gave the recurring sun and stars their undeviating way? Who established that whereby the moon waxes, and whereby she wanes save Thee? These things, O Great Creator! would I know, and others likewise still. This I ask thee, O Ahura! tell me aright: Who from beneath hath sustained the earth and the clouds above, that they do not fall? Who made the waters and the plants? Who to the wind has yoked on the storm-clouds, the swift and fleetest two? Who O Great Creator! is the inspirer of the good thoughts within our souls? This I ask Thee, O Ahura! tell me aright: Who, as a skillful artisan, hath made the lights and the darkness? Who, as thus skillful, hath made sleep and the zest of waking hours? Who spread the Auroras, the noontides and midnight, monitors to discerning man, duty's true guides?"[9] In a similar manner the Achaemenian kings magnify Ahura Mazda as having created heaven, earth, and man.

The idea of the universe is represented as one of intelligence and order. There is a geocentric conception of the universe. The sky is regarded as three-fold, the supreme heaven, the gloomy abyss, and

9. Ys. XLIV:3-5, Comp. Isa. XLV:7-12, 18.

that which is between these two.[10]   Above the at-
mosphere about the earth comes the celestial sphere,
in which the stars and constellations, and signs of the
Zodiac are set.   The moon and the sun are believed
to occupy spheres beyond the stars.   The abode of
Ahura Mazda is above all in the supreme heaven.
Different constellations guard the four quarters of
heaven and the zenith, and each of these is presided
over by a particular star.   Planets and shooting stars
mar the order of nature and they are regarded as
the creatures of Aharman.[11]   The laws of nature are
subject to Ahura Mazda or his agents.   He is the
Lord of law, of right order, and of righteousness.
The Zoroastrian conception of creation seems to
be rather that of a forming or shaping of pre-existent
matter, than a real creation *ex nihilo*.[12]   If this is so,
it is in contrast to the Jewish belief.

Whether the Iranians thought of the earth as
circular and flat or as spherical, is disputed, but the
former is generally believed.[13]   It was divided into
seven zones or circles.[14]   The Jews thought of the
world as a disc, and to the earthly disc, the heavenly
corresponded.[15]   It is probable that the idea of the
seven heavens in the Book of Enoch and the Testa-

10.   Bund. V:1-5, XII:1, Sh-1⌐Sh. VI:3.
11.   Bund. III:25, XXVIII:43-44, Zad-Spm, IV:3, 7.
12.   See H. T. Peck, "Semitic Theory of Creation," pp. 25-27
and notes.
13.   The question is discussed in Casartelli, "Mazd. Religion,"
p. III.
14.   Ys. XXXII: 3, Yt. VIII:40, XIII:94.
15.   Isa. XL:22, Job. XXII:14, Prov. VIII:27.

ments of the Twelve Patriarchs, may be a Persian
addition.

There is a fine description of the work of Yahveh
in creation in the second Book of Esdras[16] Yahveh
is alone supreme.   In the Iranian account of creation
there is in the earlier literature a recognition of an
evil spirit as joint creator with Ahura Mazda.[17] This
has no parallel in the Hebrew account.   Generally,
however, in the Avesta, and in the Achaemenian inscriptions, the sole creatorship of Ahura Mazda is
affirmed, and ideal perfection is attributed to all
his works.   Here there are marked likenesses to the
Semitic theory of creation.   The order in creation,
the different periods, the supremacy of Ahura Mazda, the ideal perfection of the newly created world,
are paralleled in the legends of Genesis.[18]   It is not
likely that the similar ideas of creation in the Avesta
were due to Jewish influence.[19]   It seems more probable that the cosmogonic conceptions of both Persians and Jews were more or less fixed before they
came into contact with each other.   The Persian
ideas of a fall and of a flood suggest Hebrew conceptions.[20]   But no more so than parallel ideas among
other peoples.   We may very reasonably suppose
that the theories of creation, the fall, and the flood

16.   II Esdras, III:1-6, 38-59.
17.   Ys. XXX.
18.   Gen. I-II 4a, II 4b-7.
19.   As Spiegel and Darmsteter, holding a late origin of the
Avesta.
20.   Bund. XV and Gen. III; Bund. VII, VI, II:21-43 and
Gen. VI:14, VIII:13.

in the Semitic and Aryan races had a common origin, and that their point of union lies behind any written history. The very dissimilarities in the theories argue their common origin, rather than that one copied from the other.[21]

As to ideas of anthropology, the Iranians believed that Gayomard, the progenitor of the race, when dying, killed by Aharman,[22] emitted his semen, and from this there developed two beings who became the parents of mankind. Their first offspring were twins, male and female, which they devoured, but they suffered their following seven pairs of children to live. From those seven pairs the whole human family descended.[23] The Hebrew narrative in comparison with this is simplicity itself.[24]

The people of the *Avesta* regarded man as consisting of body and soul, the material and the spiritual. The body is composed of numerous constituents and members. Flesh, skin, bone, blood, fat are designated, and many parts of the body are named. The spiritual element of man exists previously to the material, and does not perish like the latter at death. The life of the individual in the hereafter will be discussed later. Generally five spiritual faculties of man are recognized.[25] These are: spirit,

21. It has been thought unnecessary to review the Biblical account of creation, as the facts are so familiar as to suggest themselves.
22. Page 78.
23. Bund. III :17, 19-23, XV :1, 31, XXIV :1.
24. Gen. II :7, 18-25.
25. Ys. XXVI :4, 6, Yt. XIII :149.

reason, which watches over the corporeal functions
of man, and probably is the least of the faculties of
the soul; conscience, guarding the moral life of man;
consciousness, or perception; the soul which gives
freedom of the will, or the power of choice; and
the Fravashi or guardian spirit. The Zoroastrian
faith and philosophy recognized man's responsibility
and accountability as will be pointed out under another heading.

In the Jewish conception of man the duality[26] of
his being is assumed throughout. His body is the
physical mass in the same sense in which the Zoroastrians understood it. His soul is the inseparable
accompaniment of life with all its functions. The
word spirit as a part of human nature is very nearly
identical with that of soul.[27] A division of inward
faculties is implied.[28] Conscience, moral affections,
free-will and intellect are everywhere recognized.
As many as seven spirits are spoken of in Apocryphal
literature as being in man.[29] Many terms are used,
however, which do not indicate faculties of the soul.

26. Gen. II :7, II Esdras III :5.
27. Prov. XXV :28, XVI :32, Eccle. VII :9, II Macc. III :24.
28. Prov. XVI :2.
29. Test. Patriarchs, Reub. II :3, also Exo. XXVIII :3, Macc.
V :14, Ki. XII :22, Job XX :3, Psa. LI :10, 11, Prov. XVI :18, 32,
Isa. XI :2, LXVI :2, Zech. XII :1, 10.

CHAPTER VI

THE EXPECTATION OF A REDEEMER

IN the Zoroastrian creed the term Saoshyant is used to denote priest, deliverer, Saint.[1] It designates
the leader of the goodly company who will aid at
the general resurrection in renovating the world. The
birth of the Saviour, Soashyant, is miraculous. "Zaratust went near unto his wife Hvov three times,
and each time the seed went to the ground; the
angel Neryosang received the brilliance and strength
of that seed, delivered it with care to the angel
Anahid, and in time will blend it with a mother.
Nine thousand, nine hundred and ninety-nine, and
nine myriads of the guardian spirits of the righteous
are entrusted with its protection, so that the demons
may not injure it."[2]   The seed is preserved in Lake
Kasava, till at the end of the earthly cycle, the maid
Eredat-fedhri, bathing in the lake will conceive by
that seed and bring forth the Saviour, Saoshyant.
His two fore-runners, Ukhshyat-ereta and Ukhshyat-
Nemah, will be born in the same way of Srutat-fedhri
and Vanghu-fedhri.[3]

"The victorious Saoshyant with his helpers shall
restore the world, which henceforth never will grow
old and never die, never decaying and never rotting,
ever living and ever increasing, and master of its

1. Ys. XLVIII:9, Visp. V:1, Yt. XI:17, Ys. XLVI:3.
2. Bund. XXXII:8, 9. Yt. XIII:62.
3. Yt. XIII:141-142. Vd. XIX:5.

wish, when the dead will rise, when life and immortality will come, and the world will be restored at its wish; when the creation will grow deathless,— the prosperous creation of the Good Spirit,—and the Drug shall perish, though she may rush on every side to kill the holy beings; she and her hundred-fold brood shall perish, as it is the will of the Lord."[4]   In bringing to pass the wonderful and happy future, Saoshyant will be assisted by fifteen men and fifteen damsels. Together they perform a final sacrifice, the virtue of which will bring about the resurrection and the blessings of immortality. There will be a long conflict with evil but Saoshyant will be victorious.[5]

Are we to suppose that any of these conceptions were borrowed from Judaism? In the earliest Iranian literature there is expressed the hope of a coming Saviour.[6] The idea is certainly Zoroastrian. The worshipping Magi that centuries later came from the East to honor the Babe of Bethlehem were familiar with the conception. There are striking resemblances to the Judaeo-Christian ideas. The conquering Saoshyant is preceded by two personages who prepare the way, he is born of a virgin mother, who conceives him in a miraculous manner. His coming will bring immortality to the righteous, de-

4. Yt. XIX:89-90, 92-96, cf. Yt. XIII:129, Dk. VII:8:55, Bund. XXX:4-33.

5. Bund. XXX:17-33. Ys. XLV:11.

6. Ys. XLV:11, XLVI:3, XLVIII:9, LIII:2, XII:7, XIX:20, LIX:28.

struction to the powers of evil, and will establish the sole sovereignty of Ahura Mazda.

Parallel conceptions are found in individual prophets, but they do not represent the beliefs of the Jewish people. The earlier Jewish ideas of a Messiah were political and temporal. When in later times, ideal and spiritual conceptions are more frequently found, they do not even then displace the hopes of a political and temporal Saviour. The expectations centre about the nation. The deliverer is to be an ideal King and the viceroy of Yahveh. From their rulers they had realized only a partial good. As the years passed the fascination of the Messianic hope grew more hallowed and became the deepest passion in the heart of the nation. For a time Cyrus seemed to fulfil the role of deliverer. Zerubbabel in his turn became the centre of Messianic hopes. Simon Maccabaeus was made high-priest-king, "until there should arise a faithful prophet."[7] Feeling themselves to be without any present, the Jewish people threw themselves on the future. In contrast with this, the Zoroastrian conception of a Messiah, Saoshyant, who will give immortality and blessedness to all the righteous, is a lofty and spiritual hope.

With the Jews, a spiritual interpretation of the Messianic hope was confined to the prophets and a few devout children of Yahveh. In following the expression of this hope, truth rather than theological

7. Macca. XIV:41.

prepossession is to be our guide. The spiritual and universal elements were only slowly recognized. The happy future of the righteous in contrast with the appalling misery of the wicked, through the coming of the Messiah, was a late doctrine with the masses of the people.[8] It is probable that the Zoroastrian faith, may have had influence in bringing this belief into prominence. A striking passage is in the book of Enoch. It is in answer to the question, who was the son of man. "This is the Son of man, to whom righteousness belongs, with whom righteousness has dwelt; and who will reveal all the treasures of that which is concealed; for the Lord of spirits has chosen Him. This Son of man whom thou beholdest, shall raise up kings and the mighty from their couches, and the powerful from their thrones; shall loosen the bridles of the powerful, and break in pieces the teeth of sinners."[9] The date of this passage has been questioned, yet it probably was written in pre-christian times.[10]

A Redeemer who would rule in righteousness and bring peace to earth, was promised by Jewish prophets, but he was expected to be a national hero who would deliver Israel first. The nations were to be blessed through Israel and Israel's Redeemer.

8. II Esdras II:34, XII:32-34, Enoch LX:4-10, 14-18, Enoch LXVI:4, LXVIII:35-37, 39-41, LXX:22-24, Dan. VII:9, 13, 18, 22, 27.
9. Enoch XLVI:1-3, XLVII:3-4, L-LI.
10. A. Edersheim, "Life of Jesus," vol. I, pg. 173 n3.

CHAPTER VII

CIVIL, SOCIAL AND CEREMONIAL REGULATIONS

TO make an extended comparison between Zoroastrianism and Judaism in their social customs, and civil and ceremonial laws would be most interesting. The material is abundant, and the field almost untouched. We are aiming, however, to place the two religious systems in comparison, rather than to give an exhaustive treatment of any one idea or principle in the two religions. Under this heading, therefore, the comparisons made should be taken as suggestive only. Our treatment will be brief, with only a few selected details.

CIVIL LAWS. In treating of the legal usuages of the Avestan people it is difficult if not impossible always to separate them from the rules of the priesthood. The people of the *Avesta* are settled agriculturalists. The family forms the unit of the political organization. The clan is made up of a number of families, while the tribe is formed of a number of clans. Little is said of a political body in the early literature.[1] The master of the house, the clan-lord, tribe-lord, and chieftain of the land are recognized as having authority in their respective spheres.[2] "Good kings and evil monarchs" are sharply dis-

1. Ys. XXX :3, 4, XLIX :7, XXXI :16, Yt. X :29, 87.
2. Ys. IX :27, XIX :18, Yt. X :17-18, Vsp. III :2, Vd VII :41.

tinguished.[3]   The aim of the literature is religious, therefore little attention is paid to civil regulations. These are brought under ceremonial rules, and represent the views of the sacerdotal class. They will be treated later.   The same is true of secular laws in Judaism.   In the Persian government there was a council of state composed of the seven princes who "see the king's face."[4]   Perhaps the seven princes were regarded as representing the seven Amesha Spenta.   In the administration there were satraps and prefects, necessitating the employment of posts and means of conveyance.   A vivid picture of such an organization is given in Esther.[5]   Herodotus says of the system, "nothing mortal travels so fast."[6] Twelve parts of the armour of soldiers are enumerated in one section of the Avesta.[7]   A Pahlavi passage spiritualizes the armour of a warrior in a manner worthy of comparison with the familiar Biblical passage.[8]   The Jews, on the other hand, though they had had many warriors and an organized kingdom were not in a real sense political.   The determinative element was religious.   Their state was a theocracy, their laws were religious and ceremonial.

CASTE.   There was no rigid caste system either in

3. Ys. XLVIII :5, 10.
4. Ezra VII :14, Esther I :14.
5. Esther VIII :9-10.
6. Herod VIII :98.
7. Vd. XIV :9, also Yt. XIII :71-72, and Herod VII :61. Vd. XVII :10, Yt. I :18-19, X :39-40, 128-132.
8. Main. Kh. XLIII :7-13, with Isa. LIX :17, Eph._VI :14-17.

Zoroastrianism or in Judaism. But there were classes or orders among the people. The division of the people into priests, warriors, and tillers of the soil frequently is met with in the *Avesta*. The institution of these separate orders is traced to Zarathustra. He is distinctly called the first Priest, the first Warrior, and the first Plougher of the ground.[9] In the Bundehesh, the three sons of Zarathustra are connected with these three classes. The first was the head of the priests. The second was the commander-in-chief in war. The third was the chief of the agricultural population.[10] These orders were not castes, for they were not hereditary, nor was intermarriage forbidden. The three orders are blended by all being derived from Zarathustra. It is implied that a son in any class might be born in the same home.[11]

An artisan class is also sometimes mentioned.[12] Labor was held in respect. By cultivating a field a man was performing a religious act to the glory of Ahura Mazda. There probably was a servile class, which may have been composed only of captives taken in war. But it seems likely too that a free man might pawn away his freedom.[13] The spirit and character of the Zoroastrian faith however is against slavery.

9. Yt. XIII :88-89.
10. Bund. XXXII :5.
11. Ys. XI :6.
12. Ys. XIX :17-18, Herod I :125, 101.
13. Vd. IV :2.

These ideas are similar to those in Judaism. In the earlier days the Jews were a nomadic people. They developed into an agricultural and commercial race. There was no warrior class in Judaism. The priesthood stands distinct as an institution, but was not absolutely exclusive. There were Hebrew slaves, but their subjection was limited in time.[14] Slavery was a temporary expedient.

THE PLACE OF WOMAN. The position of woman among the Iranian people was in no way a degrading one. The good deeds of women are alluded to in the same manner as the good deeds of men.[15] There are just men and just women,[16] male and female saints.[17] We find the names of women immortalized for the good they have done.[18] The prayers of bad women are of no avail.[19] In order to marry, the girl should be past her fifteenth year.[20] A wife is an honor to the house.[21] She must be pure and her reputation unstained.[22] She is the mistress of the house, just as the husband is the master of the house.[23] She is not his slave but his companion. A maiden longs for a husband, and one who is young, strong, and learn-ed.[24] But when Zarathustra is represented as asking

14. Deut. XV:12, Lev. XXV:39. Deut. XXIII:15.
15. Ys. I:16, XIII:7, Yt. XIII:154, also Herod II:1.
16. Ys. VIII:3, XVI:9, LXXI:10, LXVIII:12-13.
17. Ys. VII:27, LVIII:5.
18. Yt. XIII:139-140, 148-149, Ys. XXXVI:8.
19. Yt. XVII:54, 57.
20. Vd. XIV:15.
21. Vd. III:3.
22. Vd. XIV:15.
23. Vd. XII:7, Gals. IV:9.
24. Yt. V:87, XV:40, Vd III:24.

to see the face of the maid, whom his father sought as bride for him, "whether its appearance be desirable, the bride turned away her face from him."[25]

Probably the marriage relation often was founded on love and piety. Perhaps the following may have been an old marriage formula: "Monitions for the marrying. I speak to you maidens, to you, I who know them; and heed ye my sayings: By these laws of the faith which I utter, obtain ye the life of the Good Mind on earth and in heaven. And to you bride and bridegroom, let each one the other in Righteousness cherish; thus alone unto each shall the home-life be happy."[26] There seems to be no evidence against the practice of polygamy. Yet monogamy seems sometimes implied.[27] Children were looked upon as a blessing, and it was a calamity and a sign of impiety to be childless.[28]

In Judaism, the position of woman generally was lower than that of man, but she had a large degree of freedom. She was looked upon as her husband's property.[29] There was always a high conception of the purity of woman.[30] Evil women are denounced for introducing foreign worship, a fact which also indicates their influence.[31] In the marriage relation

25. Zad-Spm. XX:12.
26. LV:5, also 3-4.
27. Bund. XXX:26, and most of above references.
28. Ys. XI:3, Yt. XV:40, Darius in the Behistum Inscription prays that the enemies of Ahura Mazda may be childless.
29. Exo. XX:17, Deut. V:31.
30. Lev. XVIII, XXI: 7, 9, Jer. XIII:27, Ezek. XVI:15, Isa. LVII:3 ff, et al.
31. Ezek. VIII:14, Jer. VII:18, XLIV:15, II Ki. XXIII:7.

"a virtuous woman was a crown to her husband,"[32] and the ideal is that she was to be his companion.[33] Monogamy was the general practice. Children were a delight to a home, and the childless wife was an object of reproach.[34]

RELIGIOUS VIRTUES. More will be said of religious virtues later, when morals and ethics are treated. Here some of the external elements more commonly called virtues will be pointed out. The religion of Zarathustra is a religion of culture, of spiritual and moral progress. It was a religion of energy and action, a religion of thrift. Every daily duty was sacred. Poverty and asceticism have no place among its virtues. There was an obligation to help those within the faith, but not the impious or strangers.[35]

Charity was extended to the brute creation, provided they belong to the species created by Ahura Mazda. If any of them were provoked, their complaints would be heard in heaven. The twenty-ninth Yasua contains the lament of the kine, and assurance is given of better treatment through the work of Zarathustra. The dog, too, receives special religious care and attention.[36] The clearing and cultivation of the soil, and the tending of flocks are viewed from the standpoint of religious duty.[37]

32. Prov. XII:4, XXXI:10.
33. Mal. II:14, Deut. XIII:6, Prov. XV:17, Joel I:8.
34. Psa. CXXVII:5, CXXVIII:3, Prov. XVII:6.
35. Vd. IV:1, 49, III:34-35, XVIII:12, Ys. XXXIV:5, LIII:8.
36. Vd. XIII, XV:20-51.
37. Ys. XXIX:6, XXXI:9-10, Vd. III:23, 30-32.

"Zarathustra nourished the poor, foddered the cattle, brought firewood to the fire."[38]

The propagation of the religion is a part of its essence.[39] At the same time there is an intense hatred against the wicked which is parallel to ideas often found in the Old Testament.[40] Much of the *Vendidad* is devoted to fighting and defeating the daevas.

The Jews did not carry their religion to such an extent as the Zoroastrians into their daily duties, or into their treatment of animals. Some animals were more sacred than others, but not in the sense in which the Zoroastrians understood the animal creation, as creatures of Ahura Mazda and creatures of Angro-Mainyu. The mention of dogs in the later literature may probably be due to Persian influence.[41] The dog among the Jews, however, was an unclean animal. All animals that do not have cloven hoofs and do not chew the cud were impure.[42] In Judaism kindness was to be shown to the whole animal creation. All land was recognized as belonging to Yahveh, and to be cultivated and held in trust for Him. The poor were to receive special attention, and provision was made for the care of the stranger. Almsgiving was an obligation. The book of Tobit may be called a book on almsgiving.[43] Persian influence may account

38. Zad-Spm. XX:15-16.
39. Ys. XXVIII:5.
40. Ys. XXXI:18, 20, XLIII:8, XLIV:14-15, XLV:7, XLVI:4-6, 11, et al, Psa. XCIV:1-5, 23, CXLV:20, et al.
41. Psa. LIX:14-15, Deut. XXIII:18, Job. V:16, Ecclus. XIII:17-18.
42. Lev. XI, Deut. XIV.
43. See Tobit. and Ecclus. III:30, XII:3.

for much of this.

RULES FOR PURIFICATION AND CONCERNING DEFILEMENT. The whole life of the faithful Zoroastrian was a conflict with the powers of darkness, with Angro Mainyu and his demons. Among the means of succor that Ahura Mazda gives, is the holy word revealed to Zarathustra and the prayers taught him.[44] Among the most often repeated and most highly valued forms of prayer is the Ahuna-vairya, the prayer Ahura Mazda is said to have pronounced before "the sky, before the waters, before the land, before the cattle and the plants," and before mankind existed. This prayer was recited by Zarathustra,[45] and was to be recited by men as long as the earth existed.

There were prayers for daily duties,[46] and prayers for different forms of purification.[47] Often the prayers were to be repeated and sometimes repeated many times. The words themselves were thought to contain some strange, almost magical power, and the faultless recitation of them was believed to be efficacious. Fire was the holiest and purest element, the reflection of Ahura Mazda, and symbol of moral purity. It was always a means of defence against the demons, and during the night, when they are at work, its light would frighten them away. "And we pray likewise for thy fire, O Ahura! strong through

44. Vd. XIX:2, 9, Ys. LV:2.
45. Ys. XIX:1-15, IX:14.
46. Vd. XVIII:43, 49, XVII:7.
47. VIII:19, XI, XII, XIX:22.

righteousness as it is, most swift, most powerful to
the house with joy receiving it, in many ways our
help, but to the hater, O Mazda! it is a steadfast·
harm as if with weapons hurled from the hands."[48]

Prayers and the fire were among the means of
purification. The formalities and ceremonies of
purification were multiplied to an almost endless extent. The rites were long and frequent, and complex
by many manual acts and incantations. Impurity
often came from contact with an impure body. Not
only men, but beasts and even utensils might be pol-
luted. The manner and degrees of pollution are
pointed out in detail in the *Avesta.* ·The purification
of the land, of utensils and clothes, of animals, of
women after their menses and childbirth, of men
for every pollution is prescribed by elaborate rules.
The Vendidad, the religious code of the Zoroastrians, is more minute than the Jewish Leviticus.[49]
The priests had a high place in the Iranian faith.
They kept the sacred fire, performed purification
acts, and fulfilled sacrificial function.[50] Offerings
consisted of flowers, bread, fruit, perfumes, and
there were also animal sacrifices.[51] Herodotus rec-
ognizes these, and at the same time he say's the Persians "had no images, no temples and no altars."[52]

48. XXXIV:4. See also Vd. XVIII:18-23, 27, VIII:73 ff,
Ys. LXII, XVII:11, Bund. XVII:5-8.
49. See Vendidad.
50. Vd. XVIII:1-6, IX:47, 49.
51. Yt. V:21, 25, 29, 107, 108, 112, 116, IX:3, 8, 13 Yt. XV:7,
15, Yt. XVII:24, 28, Vd. XVIII:70, XXII:3-4.
52. Herod I:131-132.

This was mainly true, though the Persians had altars which were sometimes covered.

The priests were to maintain their authority. They were to inflict punishment for transgressions against the ritual and ceremonial laws. It is striking that for almost every law given in the Vendidad, there is added at the same time the punishment that shall be inflicted upon the guilty in case of transgression. The stereotyped expression for a man's committing transgression is, "what is the penalty that he shall pay."[53] The germs and general ideas of the system thus elaborated in the later *Avesta,* are distinctly found in the Gathas.[54] But in the *Gathas* the conceptions are more mental and spiritual.

In Judaism, the manner and times of prayer were sometimes exactly parallel to Zoroastrian habits,[55] and they equally covered nearly every event of life. With the Jews fire was sacred but not in the sense in which the Zoroastrians held it. It was to have been always kept burning in the temple.[56] It was a symbol of Yahveh,[57] and a means of purification. The work of the priests, and the ceremonial regulations, were elaborate and more strictly defined in the Persian period than they had been before. Cleanness or uncleanness was applied to land,

53. Vd. III:36 seq. V:14, 43, VI:4, VIII:24, XVIII:67.
54. Ys. XXXIV:6, XLV:6, 8, 10, L:4, 9.
55. Dan. VI:10, Psa. LV:17, LXXXVIII:13, CXIX:147, I Ki. VIII:48.
56. Lev. VI:12-13.
57. Exo. III:2, XIII:21, XIX:18, Dan. VII:9-10, Mal. III:2, II Macca. I:18-35.

dwellings, clothes, utensils, animals, men and women, and strict minute laws of purification were enforced. Religious offerings might include a great number of objects, as in the Zoroastrian faith. There were punishments prescribed for every violation of the ritual and ceremonial law. A comparison between the purification laws in the two religions shows many striking resemblances. The effect of the presence of, or the contact with, the dead is a single illustration. The Zoroastrians, however, carried their laws concerning the dead, as well as many other purification and ceremonial laws to much greater lengths than the Jews.[58]

The rapid development in post-exilic times of the ritualistic and ceremonial regulations, that so characterized later Judaism, we must attribute in part to the rigorous observance by the Persians of more stringent laws and rites. Persian influence is probably responsible for Jewish ceremonialism attaining such far-reaching importance. The feast of Purrin, in honor of the deliverance from the schemes of Haman, may be an adopted Persian festival.[59]

58. Vd. VI, VII, VIII, Num. XIX:16, Jer. XVI:4, XXV:33.
59. Esther IX:17-32, II Macca. XV:36, Josephus Ant. XI:6, 13.

CHAPTER VIII

MORALS AND ETHICS

PURITY in thoughts, in words and in deeds, is a summary of the ethical life of the Zoroastrian. It includes all moral precepts. This ideal is constantly found throughout the *Avesta*. There is much externality in the Iranian religion as has been shown, already, but the subjective element is also strong. "Thou Righteousness, when shall I see thee, knowing the Good Mind, and above all the personified Obedience, which constitutes the way to the most beneficient Ahura Mazda."[2] An external offering or sacrifice is made valuable through the good thoughts, words and deeds of an individual.[3] Those who are not pure in thought are far from the Good Mind of Ahura Mazda.[4] "Any one in the world here below can win purity for himself, namely, when he cleanses himself with good thoughts, words, and deeds. The will of the Lord is the law of holiness."

"Holiness is the best of all good. Happy, happy the man who is holy with perfect holiness."[5] Many chapters of the eighth Dinkard close with the words, "Righteousness is perfect excellence."[6] In the *Gathas*

1. Ys. XXX :3, XLV :8, Vsp. II :5, Yt. V :18.
2. Ys. XXVIII :6.
3. Ys. XXXIV :3, Gah. IV :9, Yt. XXII :14.
4. Ys. XXXIV :8.
5. Vd. X :18-20, XIX :22.
6. Dk. VIII :2 :5, 7 :24, et al.

Ahura Mazda, in response to prayer, is able to give "helpful grace" and "meet the spirit's need."[7]   In the ten admonitions given in a chapter of the Pahlavi literature is the following, "keep the way of the good open to your house, for the sake of making righteousness welcome in your abode."[8]

Love of truth is a characteristic of those in the Iranian faith. Nothing is more shameful than a lie. "The man of truth shall be more resplendent than the sun; the man of a lie goeth straightway to the demon whence he cometh."[9] Such lofty conceptions· implied benevolence, charity, uprightness, eschewing of deceit and theft, purity of body as well as soul, temperance, restraint, and these are all in the teachings of the faith.

As Ahura Mazda looks upon the smallest sin with displeasure, so Yahveh knows the secrets of all hearts.[10]   The high moral conceptions of deity exalted the moral standards of the people. Among the Zoroastrians, morality was identified with the holy will of Ahura Mazda, and among the Jews with the holy will of Yahveh. The character of Yahveh was the final rule for men.[11] The philosophy of the Wisdom Books reaches the same conclusion that it was "the whole of man" to "fear Yahveh and keep

7. Ys. XLVI :2.
8. Zad-Spm. XXIV :10-19, also XXI-15-16, 18.
9. Herod I :138, 183, Vd. IV :1-2, Sik-G-Vig VIII :128-130, Ys. XXXI :2.
10. Ys. XXXI :13, and Psa. CXXXIX, XLIV :21, I Chron. XXIX :9.
11. Psa. XVIII :25-26, XXV :8-10, XXXIII :5, XCVII :10-12.

His commandments."[12]   The will of Yahveh had been announced by priests and prophets, and then came to be embodied in the legal codes.

In pre-exilic times the ethical standards of the people were extremely low.   The few writers who have higher conceptions, give little prominence to the inward life.   The sins are mostly external and national.   The Deuteronomist, Jeremiah and Ezekiel introduce the emphasis upon the inwardness of religion.   In post-exilic times this receives its highest development in the Psalms.   The upright man is good in thought and word and deed.[13]   But much of post-exilic literature is still external in its conceptions of holiness and sin.

The ethical standard of the Zoroastrian faith is not inferior to that in Judaism.   The emphasis placed upon inwardness and spirituality in religion, even suggest whether Judaism may not have been helped to a grasping of spiritual conceptions by the followers of Zarathustra.

A primal factor of the morals and ethics of the Iranian religion is the freedom of the will.[14]   Every individual must choose to be on the side of Ahura Mazda, or on the side of Angro Mainyu, and he must fulfil the duties which are consequently imposed upon him.   Indifferentism or failure to choose is impossible.   Every good deed a man does increases

12.   Eccle. XI :13.
13.   Psa. XIX :12-14, XV :2-3, LXXVIII :17-18, LI :12-13. Deut. VI :25, Prov. IV :23, et al.
14.   Ys. XXX :2-3, XXXI :11, 20, XLVI :10-13, LI :6.

the power of good, every evil deed the power of evil. Zarathustra declared himself sent to assist men to the good.[15] Freedom to choose means responsibility. This is a strong characteristic of the religion. A strict watch is kept by the divinities over every individual, and all deeds are recorded. Even the demons were not evil by nature, but became so by choosing to place themselves in opposition to Ahura Mazda.[16] Such moral earnestness colored the whole life of the Zoroastrian. In Jewish writings there is everywhere recognized, or assumed, the same freedom of man's will. He is under no coercion. Every man is responsible for his deeds.[17] The Iranian and Jewish faiths are precisely the same in this respect.

15. Ys. XXXI:2.
16. Ys. XXX:3-6.
17. I Chron. XXVIII:9, Eccle. XI:9, Ezek. XXXIII:1-19, Mal. III:16.

CHAPTER IX

THE FUTURE LIFE

ONLY an outline treatment of the Zoroastrian and Jewish conceptions of a future life will be attempted. But sufficient for a fair comparison to be made. When death takes place the soul remains in the vicinity of the body for three days, and three nights which indicates a kind of transitional stage, during which the soul of the good man has a foretaste of the delights of Paradise and that of the evil man the torments of Hell.[1] The body becomes a prey of the demons who rejoice over its death.[2] Impurity was communicated to everything in the house, and to all who stood in any relationship to the dead. There was an elaborate series of ceremonies for purification to which reference already has been made.

After the three days and three nights during which the happy pious soul has been lingering about the body, on the dawn of the fourth day the soul passes over the Chinvat Bridge. The pious soul meets a balmy and sweet scented wind. "It seems to him as if his own conscience were advancing to him in that wind, in 'the shape of a maiden fair, bright, white-armed, strong, tall-formed, high-

1. Yt. XXII.
2. Vd. VII :2, 30, III :14, IX :40.

96

standing, thick-breasted, beautiful of body, noble, of a glorious seed, of the size of a maid in her fifteenth year, as fair as the fairest things in the world.' " In response to the soul's question as to who she is, she answers, "O thou youth of good thoughts, good words, and good deeds, of good religion, I am thine own conscience;" and then recounts the good works which the soul accomplished during its earthly career.[3]

Through three steps the faithful soul passes into the Paradise of good thoughts, of good words, and of good deeds, and at the fourth step into the Paradise of Endless Light, the House of Song, where Ahura Mazda, the holy angels and the pious dead dwell.[4]

The fate of the impious soul is altogether the opposite of this. In misery the wicked soul wanders about the corpse for three days and three nights. On the morning of the fourth day at the passage of the Chinvat Bridge, it meets a foul, chilly wind blowing from the north. In that wind the soul perceives its own conscience in the shape of an ugly hag. In answer to the soul's question she declares she is the embodiment of his evil thoughts, words, and deeds, and recites his wickedness upon earth. Through three successive steps, the evil soul passes into the place of evil thoughts, evil words, evil deeds, and last of all into the region of eternal darkness, which

3. Yt. XXII:9-14, Diu. Main Kd. II:114-143.
4. Yt. XXII:15, III:4, Vd. XIX:36, Din. M-Kd. II:145-157, Ys. LI:13, 15, XXXI:21, XLV:8.

is most foul and full of suffering, and the abode of Angro Mainyu and his followers.[5]

There is conceived to be a private judgment in which man's conscience, personified as a beautiful maiden or a horrid hag, described above, is the judge. At the Chinvat Bridge, justice is administered to the soul before the three angels Sarosha, Mithra, and Rashnu. The good and evil deeds are weighed against each other, and decision is rendered in accordance with the turn of the scales. If the good deeds outweigh the evil ones, the soul is assisted by the angels and the beautiful maiden into Paradise. If not, he is assailed by the demons and the ugly hag and is hurried or falls down to hell. The Bridge becomes broad to the righteous soul, and so narrow to the wicked that the lost soul falls from it, and descends through successive stages into the wretched abode of Angro Mainyu.[6] In the *Gathas* the idea of a judgment dividing the good and evil is clearly conceived.[7] Throughout the *Avesta* the future condition of the soul is described as a personal, conscious experience of happiness or misery.

There is in the Iranian faith perfect confidence in Ahura Mazda's justice. If the wicked prosper in this life, it will not always be so. The faithful will

5. Yt. XXII:19-36, Din. M. Kd. II:158-194, Bund. XXVIII:47, Ard. Vf. XVII:2-27, Ys. XLVI:10-11, XLIX:11, XXXI:20, LI:14.

6. Vd. XIX:27-32, Din. M. Kd. II:115-122, 162-163, Bund. XII:7.

7. Ys. XXXIII:1-2, XXX:8-10, XLV:10-12, et al.

be delivered from all suffering and have abundant happiness in the life to come. Ahura Mazda will be absolutely just in his awards to the wicked and to the righteous, and a new order of things will be established. "I conceived of thee as bountiful, O Great Giver, Mazda! when I beheld thee as supreme in the generation of life, when, as rewarding deeds and words, thou didst establish evil for the evil, and happy blessings for the good, by thy great virtue to be adjudged to each in the creation's final change."[8] Rewards and punishments are self-induced, and this follows from the belief in individual responsibility.[9]

The happiness and misery of the next world is essentially mental and spiritual. A single illustration of the hope of the righteous will indicate this: "And now in these thy dispensations, O Ahura Mazda! do thou wisely act for us, and with abundance with thy bounty and thy tenderness as touching us; and grant that reward which thou hast appointed to our souls, O Ahura Mazda! Of this do thou thyself bestow upon us for this world and the spiritual; and now as part thereof do thou grant that we may attain to fellowship with thee, and thy righteousness for all duration."[10]

There are hints of a belief in the resurrection of the body in the *Gathas*,[11] and in all the remaining

8. Ys. XLIII :5, also 4, 6, XXX :8-10, XLV :7-8, Ys. LI :6, Yt. XIX :89.
9. Ys. XXXI :20, Ys. XLVI :11.
10. Ys. XL :1-2, also XXXI :20-21, XXXII :15, XLV :7, XLVI :10-12, 19, XLIX :11.
11. Ys. XLVI :11, XLIX :11, XLV :8.

Iranian literature it is clearly set forth. The resurrection is brought into connection with the regeneration of the world. "We sacrifice unto the kingly glory, that will cleave unto the victorious Saoshyant and his helpers, when he shall restore the world, which will thenceforth never grow old and never die, never decaying and never rotting, ever living and ever increasing, and master of its wish, when the dead will rise, when life and immortality will come, and the world will be restored."[12] At the coming and triumph of Saoshyant, a Fragment declares, "Let Angro Mainyu be hid beneath the earth. Let the daevas likewise disappear. Let the dead arise, unhindered by these foes, and let bodily life be sustained in these now lifeless bodies."[13]

The idea of the resurrection's being connected with the coming of Saoshyant and the regeneration of the world, is parallel to the hopes of *the primitive and some present day* Christians in the expected return of Christ. But the underlying features of the Zoroastrian eschatology are not late, but belong to the oldest teachings of the system. A mighty conflict precedes the end of the world. The powers of darkness are arrayed against those of light. The fiend-smiting Saoshyant will be completely victorious. He will renovate the world, make the living immortal, and cause the dead to arise. This be-

12. Yt. XIX:88-89, also 11, 19, 23.
13. Frag. IV:3. See also Bund. XXX:1, 4, Dk. IX:46, 4, Vd. XVIII:51.

lief is throughout the *Avesta*.[14]

For detail and vividness of portrayal, and for loftiness of conception, the Zoroastrian ideas of the future condition of the individual, of a judgment, of future rewards and punishments, and of a resurrection, are far in advance of anything to be found in Judaism. Until a late period, Jewish ideas upon the future life were exceedingly shadowy. The conception of Yahveh and nearness to Him, may have implied immortality and future blessedness for the faithful. That does not concern us. The Jews did not see the implication.

In nearly every religion no matter how rude, there is some suggestion of a belief in immortality, though often vague and materialistic in form. Without such a belief, "religion surely is like an arch resting on one pillar, like a bridge ending in an abyss."[15] Yet among the early Jews there is no definite teaching concerning immortality, and no hopeful view of the future life. Sheol is always spoken of with a tone of sadness. It is the final abode of all good or bad. Existence there is colorless. It is a place of silence and forgetfulness.[16] Faith in Yahveh led to individual surmises of a life after death, but these gropings are only occasional.[17] They do not repre-

14. Vd. XIX:5, Yt. XIII:129, XIX:89, 95-96. Ys. XLV:11, LIII:2, XIII:7, LIX:28.

15. F. Max Müller, *"Chips from a German Workshop,"* vol. I, p. 45.

16. Psa. LXXXVIII:12, CXV:17, Job. XIV:21.

17. Gen. V:24, II Ki. II:11, IV:35, XIII:21, I Ki. XVII:22.

sent the faith of the people. The earthly life had a strong hold upon the Jewish people. Their hopes of the future related to the enjoyment of Yahveh upon earth and to Israel's glory.

In the Persian period of Jewish writings a belief in immortality has for the first time taken definite form, and this becomes clearer in still later writings. There is a growing hope in the future life.) "This present world is not the end." "There is promised us an everlasting hope."[18] There will be happy rewards for the righteous and punishments for the wicked.[19] All men will be brought to judgment and Yahveh will be their judge.[20]

The coming of the Messiah will inaugurate a new order of things. There will be "new heavens and a new earth."[21] The righteous individual, as well as the righteous nation, will receive blessings in the Messianic kingdom, and there will be a resurrection of the dead. "Thy dead men shall live, together with my dead body shall they arise. Awake and sing, ye that dwell in dust: for thy dew is as the dew of herbs, and the earth shall cast out the dead."[22] But it is Yahveh not the Messiah who will raise the dead. In some of the Psalms there is an intimation

18. II Esdras VII:112, 120, 93-140, VIII:53-55, XIV:35.
19. Dan. XII:2-3, Enoch. XXXVIII:1-3, XC:24-26, Ecclus. IX:12, II Esdras XIV:35, Wisd. V:15-16.
20. Judith XVI:17, Dan. VII:9-10, XII:14, Psa. XCVI:13, Eccle. XI:9, Enoch X:1-10, II Esdras VII:73, 113-115, Wisd. II:22.
21. Isa. LXV:17, LXVI:18-24, Enoch LII:4, LXVI:4 seq.
22. Isa. XXVI:19, II Macc. VII:14. Which is of late origin. Dan. XII:2-3, Enoch LI:4, LXII:15-16.

that the reward of the righteous will be spiritual, that there will be mental communion with Yahveh.[23]

The direct and positive teachings concerning the future life that suddenly appear in the literature of post-exilic times are best accounted for through Zoroastrian influence. The Zoroastrian ideas of the future life probably date from not later than the fifth century B. C., as has been shown. When the Jews came into contact with the Persians holding with fervor the hope of immortality, they could not but ask themselves whether that hope was to be discovered in their own religion. Some would refuse to acknowledge that the great doctrine was a part of the faith, as the later Sadducees. But most of the people were eager to accept the new and inspiring hope. Their misfortunes made them all the more ready to believe in the life to come. As soon as the Jews felt that the hope of the future life, had been latent in their faith, and could be developed from it, they vied with the Zoroastrians in the earnestness with which they maintained it.[24]

23. Psa. XLIX:15, XVII:15, XVI:10-11, LXXIII:24-28, Josephus, Wars, II:8, 11.
24. For Jewish and Old Testament ideas of the future life, see R. H. Charles, *Eschatology*, C. H. Joy, *Judaism and Christianity*, pp. 372 seq. T. K. Cheyne in *Expository Times*, vol. II.

CHAPTER X

THE Zoroastrian faith is one of the world's great religions. The purity and ideality of Ahura Mazda, the belief in the company of holy angels that do his bidding, the expectation of a coming Saviour, the high value set upon man, the lofty conception of the future life, the final overcoming of evil by good, are among the elements of strength. The depth of its philosophy, the spirituality of many of its views, the clearness and purity of its ethics, are scarcely equalled by any creed of ancient times. In the face of these noble conceptions, it is remarkable that what is probably the purest religion of antiquity, except the Jewish, should almost have perished from the earth.

But there are some striking elements of weakness. Ahura Mazda is not almighty. The dualism is a leading feature, dualism entering into every thing in life. The influence of demons was carried to ridiculous extremes, and resembled witchcraft and enchantments. The ceremonial and ritual regulations were cumbrous, and along with lofty and profound conceptions were often puerile supersitions.

Judaism came to the conception of Yahveh as the supreme Ruler of the universe, and with that their responsibility to the nations confronted them. He

104

was no longer a tribal God. There was no god beside Him. He was supreme and righteous. The spirituality and high ideals of some of the Psalms and Deutero-Isaiah, indicate that the ritual worship and ceremonial rites were not to all empty forms.[1] But in their very forms there is a mark of strength. They preserved the worship of Yahveh, kept the Sabbaths and rest days, guarded the sacred oracles, and fostered a high morality. The rise of the synagogue worship was a valuable force in the religion. The people too cultivated love of family and of race, and their clannishness was a protection to their faith. The weakness of Judaism lay in misconceptions and diverted energies. Yahveh was thought of as Judge, and King. Only a few prayed to Him as Father and Friend. The hope of a temporal kingdom and earthly glory crowded out spiritual expectations. The ceremonial sometimes was substituted for genuine righteousness, and more often ceremonial laws and rites were absurd and harmful.

It has been pointed out already that the main elements of the Zoroastrian faith were for the most part fixed before the Persian period of Jewish history, and that there was probably no marked influence made by the Jews upon the Persian faith. The Jews, however, discovering that their rulers had many conceptions and teachings similar to, and others in advance of their own, would, in receiving

1. Psa. XL, L, LI, CXX-CXXXIV, Isa. XLVI:3, 4, 12, Isa. XLIX:15, LI, LV, LXI.

and adopting them, easily deduce such teachings and conceptions from their own revelation, with no thought that they were borrowing. At any rate, later generations would think of them as purely Jewish beliefs. While the germs of the beliefs that came into prominence in post-exilic times in Judaism may be present in the earlier writings, the germs alone are not enough to explain the later developments. The explanation is found in the fact that the "germs which lay hidden in Judaism were fertilized by contact with the Persian religion."[2] To this foreign contact, therefore, we probably are indebted for some of the loftiest and most spiritual conceptions, which came into Judaism and passed from Judaism into Christianity. The Jews were not only influenced by contact with the Persian faith, but by those who became converts to Judaism. As to-day a person changing from one faith to another decidedly different carries into the new faith some of his old influences, so the very fact that many Persians became Jews[3] would favor the development or adoption of beliefs already latent in Judaism.

The followers of the Zoroastrian faith probably furnished the stimulus for ideas and beliefs that otherwise might not have come into prominence. These beliefs Judaism preserved and fostered for fuller development under the benign influence of Christianity.

2. C. F. Kent, *The Jewish People*, p. 257.
3. Esther VIII :17.

BIBLIOGRAPHY

American Presbyterian Review, Vol. XII, pp. 281-290. *The Zoroastrian Religion.*

Academy, The. Vol. XLIII, pp. 525-527. Review of Darmesteter's *Translation of the Avesta.*

Batten, L. W. *The Social Life of the Hebrews from Josiah to Ezra*, in *Biblical World*, 11, 397-409.

Bixby, J. T. *Zoroaster and Persian Dualism*, in *The Arena*, Vol. V, pp. 694-711.

Brace, C. Louing. *The Unknown God*, pp. 41-51, pp. 182-198. *The Races of the Old World*, pp. 52-77.

Britanica, Encyclopedia, Zoroaster, Zend-Avesta, Purim, Persepolis, Persia, Cosmogony.

Carus, Paul. *Mazdaism*, in *The Open Court*, Vol. II, pp. 141-149.

Casartelli, L. C. *The Philosophy of the Mazday-asnian Religion under the Sassanids.*

Cassel, Paulus. *Commentary on Esther;* appendix, *Zoroaster.*

Charles, R. H. *Eschatology, or The Doctrine of a Future Life.*

Cheyne, T. K. *Possible Zoroastrian Influences on the Religion of Israel*, in the *Expository Times*, Vol. II, pp. 202-209, 224-228, 248-254. *The Origin of the Psalter*, pp. 255-306, 381-447.

The Book of Psalms, in *Semitic Studies*, pp. 111-119. *Jewish Religious Life After the Exile*, pp. 74, 210, 251-261.

Christian Remembrances, The Zend-Avesta, Vol. XLIX, pp. 451-474.

Clarke, J. F. *Ten Great Religions*, Vol. I, pp. 171-208. Vol. II, pp. 58, 91, 130-134, 209.

Cobbe, F. P. *Studies New and Old of Ethical and Social Subjects*, pp. 89-147.

Cornill, Carl H. *The Prophets of Israel*, pp. 17-30.

Cox, F. A. *The Manners and Customs of the Israelites.*

Darmesteter. *The Zend-Avesta, in Sacred Books of the East*, Vols. IV and XXIII.

Eclectic Magazine. Vol. XIV, pp. 476-489. *Zoroaster and the Persian Fire Worshippers.*

Edersheim, A. Life of Jesus. Appendix XIII.

Ewald, H. *Old and New Testament Theology*, pp. 72-78.

Fenton, John. *Early Hebrew Life.*

Fluegel, Maurice. *The Zend-Avesta and Eastern Religions.*

Fuller, J. M. *The Angelology of the Book of Daniel*, in *Bible Commentary*, Vol. VI, pp. 348-351.

Geiger, A. *Judaism and its History*, pp. 127-132.

Geiger, W. *Civilization of the Eastern Iranians*, translated by D. D. P. Sanjana, 2 Vols., *Zarathustra in the "Gathas,"* translated by D. D. P. Sanjanna, pp. 1-65, 206-256.

Goldziher, Ignez. *Mythology Among the Hebrew*, pp. 326-329.

Gottheil, R. J. *Classical Studies in Honor of Henry Drisler*, pp. 24-51, 94-125.

Graetz, H. *History of the Jews*, Vols. I and II.

Hardwick, Charles. *Christ and Other Masters*, Vol. II, pp. 361-439.

Harpers Classical Dictionary. *Zoroaster. Rhagae.*

Harper, E. T. *Historical Movements in Israel From the Reform of Josiah to the Second Temple*, in *Biblical World*, 382-396.

Hastings Bible Dictionary, *God, Cosmogony, Angels, Demons, Ethics.*

Haug, M. *Essays on The Sacred Language, Writing and Religion of the Parsees. Zoroaster and Zoroastrianism* in *Methodist Quarterly Review*, Vol. XLI, pp. 61-77.

Hausrath, Adolph. *History of New Testament Times*, Vol. I, pp. 84-93, 135-173.

Herodotus. Translated by G. Rawlinson, Vols. I and II, Books I and III.

History for Ready Reference, Vol. V, pp. 3666-3668. *Zoroastrianism.*

Hunter, P. H. *After the Exile*, Vols. I and II.

Jackson, A. V. W. *The Ancient Persian Doctrine of a Future Life*, in *Biblical World*, Vol. VIII, pp. 149-163. *Zoroaster the Prophet of Iran. The Moral and Ethical Teachings of the Zoroastrian Religion*, in *International Journal of Ethics*, Vol. VII, pp. 55-62. *Ormazd, or the*

Ancient Persian Idea of God, in *The Monist*, Vol. IX, pp. 161-178. *Doctrine of the Resurrection Among the Ancient Persians*, in *American Oriental Society Journal*, Vol. XVI, pp. 38-39. *A New Reference in the Avesta to the "Life Book" Hereafter*, in *A. O. S. J.*, Vol. XIV, pp. 20-21. *Avestan Superstitions*, in *A. O. S. J.*, Vol. XIII, pp. 59-61. *The Ancient Persian Abhorrence of Falsehood*, in *A. O. S. J.*, Vol. XIII, pp. 102-103. *An Vestan Grammar.* Introduction. *Avesta the Bible of Zoroaster*, in *Biblical World*, Vol. I, pp. 420-431.

Johnson, Samuel, Rev. *Oriental Religious-Persia.*

Johnson's Univ, Ency. Avesta, Ahriman, Iranian, Ormazd, Pahlavi, Zoroaster.

Josephus, Flavius. *Antiquities of the Jews.* Books XI-XIII.

Karaka, Dosabhai F. *History of the Parsis*, Vol. I and II.

Kent, C. F. *A History of the Jewish People.*

Kohut, Alexander. *"Judische Angelologie und Dämonologie." Zoroastrian Legends and their Biblical Sources*, in *N. Y. Independent*, Mch. 19, 1891. *The Zend-Avesta and the First Eleven Chapters of Genesis*, in *Jewish Quarterly Review*, Vol. II, pp. 223-229. *Parsic and Jewish Legends of The First Man*, in *Jewish Quarterly Review*, Vol. III, pp. 231-250.

Knenen, A. *The Religion of Israel*, Vol. II, p. 156, and Vol. III.

Lazarus, M. E. *The Zend-Avesta and Solar Religions.*

Lenormant, Francois. *Ancient History of the East.* Vol. II, pp. 21-40. *The Beginnings of History*, pp. 59-61, 109-111, 272, 429-431.

Maspero, G. *The Passing of the Empires*, pp. 571-601, 629-639.

McClintock and Strong's Bib. and Theo. Ency. Parsees and *Persia.*

McCurdy, J. F. *Josiah to Ezra in Bib. World*, Vol. II, pp. 369-381.

Meyer, Edward. *"Geschichte des Alterthums,"* Vols. I, II.

Mills, L. H. *The Zend-Avesta, The Zend-Avesta*, in *S. B. E.*, Vol. XXXI. *Asha as the Law in the "Gathas"* in *Amer. Oriental Society Journal*, Vol. XX, pp. 31-53. *The Initiative of the Avesta*, in *R. A. S. Journel*, Vol. LI, pp. 271-294. *Immortality in the "Gathas"* in *The Thinker*, Vol. II, pp. 104-112. *The God of Zoroaster*, in *The New World*, Vol. IV, pp. 47-56. *The Five Zarathustrian "Gathas."*

Mitchell, J. M. *Methodist Quarterly Review*, Vol. XXXIX, pp. 114-133.

Modi, Jinanji, J. *The Religious System of the Parsees*, in *The World's Parliament of Religions*, Vol. II, pp. 898-920.

Montefiore, C. G. *The Religion of the Ancient Hebrews.*

Moulton, J. H. *Zoroaster and Israel*, in *The*

Thinker. Vol. I, pp. 401-408, Vol. II, 308-315, 490-501.

Muller, Max F. *Chips From a German Workshop,* Vol. I, pp. 45, 115-178. *Origin and Growth of Religion,* pp. 125-127. *Sacred Books of the East,* Vols. IV, V, XVIII, XXIII, XXIV, XXXI, XXXVII, XLVII. *James Darmesteter and His Studies in Zend Literature,* in *Jewish Quarterly Review,* Vol. VII, pp. 173-195.

Nation, The. Review of Mill's Translation of the *Avesta,* Vol. XLVII, p. 37.

National Quarterly Review, The. Zoroaster as a Legislator and Philosopher, Vol. XXXII, pp. 1-25.

Paton, L. B. *The Religion of Judah From Josiah to Ezra* in *Biblical World,* Vol. XI, pp. 410-421.

Peck, H. T. *The Semitic Theory of Creation,* pp. 22-27.

Pressensé, Edmund de. *The Religions Before Christ,* pp. 35-44, 191-238.

Prince, J. Dynely. *Commentary on the Book of Daniel, pp.* 116-122, 170-171.

Pusey, E. B. *Daniel the Prophet,* pp. 498-568.

Ragozin, Zenaide A. *The Story of Media, Babylon, and Persia.*

Rawlinson, G. *Historical Illustrations of the Old Testament,* pp. 174-209. *The Religions of the Ancient World,* pp. 77-105. *The Five Great*

Monarchies of the Ancient Eastern World, Vol.
III, pp. 73-240. Vol. IV. *The Sixth Monarchy*, pp. 398-402. *The Seventh Monarchy*,
pp. 621-656. *Herodotus*, Vols. I and II, Books
I and II.

Rawlinson, H. C. *Cuneiform Inscriptions at Behistun, Persepolis, etc., in Roy. As. Soc. Journal*,
Vol. X.

Renan, Ernest. *History of the People of Israel*,
Vols. III and IV.

Sanjana, D. D. P. *The Position of Zoroastrian
Women in Remote Antiquity.* See also W.
Geiger.

Sayce, A. H. *Origin and Growth of Religion*, pp.
89-91.

Schodde, G. H. *The Development of New Testament Judaism*, in *Bibliothecra Sacra*, Vol. L,
pp. 193-219.

Schurer, Emil. *History of the Jewish People in the
Time of Jesus Christ;* Division 2, Vol. II.

Smith, G. A. Isaiah, Vol. II, pp. 57-65, 162-173.

Smith, J. A. *The Iranian Scripture* in *The Chau-
tauquan*, Vol. VIII, pp. 400-402.

Spiegel, F. Von. *The Avesta, the Religious Books
of the Parsees.*

Stifler, J. M. *Does Christianity Displace Judaism*,
in *Bib. Sacra*, Vol. LIII, pp. 691-707.

Tiele, C. P. *The History of Religion*, 160-179.

Toy, Crawford, H. *Judaism and Christianity.* ——

Tylor, E. B. *Primitive Culture*, Vol. II, pp. 19-22.

Upham, F. W. *The Wise Men.*

Unitarian Magazine. *The Religion of Zoroaster,* Vol. XXIX, pp. 122-138.

Warner's Library of World's Best Lit. Avesta.

West, E. W. Translation of *Pahlavi Texts in Sacred Books of the East,* Vols. V, XVIII, XXIV, XXXVII and XLVII. *Zarathustra's Doctrine Regarding the Soul* in *R. A. S. J.,* Vol. 605-611.

Whitney, W. D. *Oriental and Linguistic Studies,* pp. 149-198.

Wilson, J. *The Parsi Religion.*

Xenophon. *The Anabasis.*

INDEX

Bringing Classics to Life

BOOK JUNGLE

www.bookjungle.com *email: sales@bookjungle.com fax: 630-214-0564 mail: Book Jungle PO Box 2226 Champaign, IL 61825*

QTY

The Two Babylons
Alexander Hislop

You may be surprised to learn that many traditions of Roman Catholicism in fact don't come from Christ's teachings but from an ancient Babylonian "Mystery" religion that was centered on Nimrod, his wife Semiramis, and a child Tammuz. This book shows how this ancient religion transformed itself as it incorporated Christ into its teachings....

Religion/History   **Pages:358**

ISBN: *1-59462-010-5*   *MSRP* **$22.95**

The Power Of Concentration
Theron Q. Dumont

It is of the utmost value to learn how to concentrate. To make the greatest success of anything you must be able to concentrate your entire thought upon the idea you are working on. The person that is able to concentrate utilizes all constructive thoughts and shuts out all destructive ones...

Self Help/Inspirational   **Pages:196**

ISBN: *1-59462-141-1*   *MSRP* **$14.95**

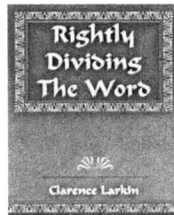

Rightly Dividing The Word
Clarence Larkin

The "Fundamental Doctrines" of the Christian Faith are clearly outlined in numerous books on Theology, but they are not available to the average reader and were mainly written for students. The Author has made it the work of his ministry to preach the "Fundamental Doctrines." To this end he has aimed to express them in the simplest and clearest manner..

Religion   **Pages:352**

ISBN: *1-59462-334-1*   *MSRP* **$23.45**

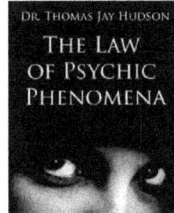

The Law of Psychic Phenomena
Thomson Jay Hudson

"I do not expect this book to stand upon its literary merits; for if it is unsound in principle, felicity of diction cannot save it, and if sound, homeliness of expression cannot destroy it. My primary object in offering it to the public is to assist in bringing Psychology within the domain of the exact sciences. That this has never been accomplished..."

New Age   **Pages:420**

ISBN: *1-59462-124-1*   *MSRP* **$29.95**

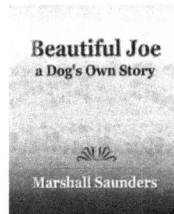

Beautiful Joe
Marshall Saunders

When Marshall visited the Moore family in 1892, she discovered Joe, a dog they had nursed back to health from his previous abusive home to live a happy life. So moved was she, that she wrote this classic masterpiece which won accolades and was recognized as a heartwarming symbol for humane animal treatment...

Fiction   **Pages:256**

ISBN: *1-59462-261-2*   *MSRP* **$18.45**

Bringing Classics to Life

BOOK JUNGLE

www.bookjungle.com *email: sales@bookjungle.com fax: 630-214-0564 mail: Book Jungle PO Box 2226 Champaign, IL 61825*

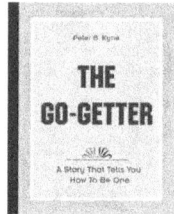

The Go-Getter
Kyne B. Peter

QTY

The Go Getter is the story of William Peck. He was a war veteran and amputee who will not be refused what he wants. Peck not only fights to find employment but continually proves himself more than competent at the many difficult test that are throw his way in the course of his early days with the Ricks Lumber Company...

Business/Self Help/Inspirational   **Pages:68**

ISBN: *1-59462-186-1*   *MSRP* ***$8.95***

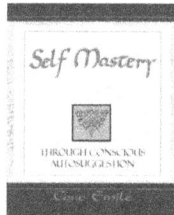

Self Mastery
Emile Coue

Emile Coue came up with novel way to improve the lives of people. He was a pharmacist by trade and often saw ailing people. This lead him to develop autosuggestion, a form of self-hypnosis. At the time his theories weren't popular but over the years evidence is mounting that he was indeed right all along...

New Age/Self Help   **Pages:98**

ISBN: *1-59462-189-6*   *MSRP* ***$7.95***

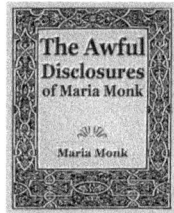

The Awful Disclosures Of
Maria Monk

"I cannot banish the scenes and characters of this book from my memory. To me it can never appear like an amusing fable, or lose its interest and importance. The story is one which is continually before me, and must return fresh to my mind with painful emotions as long as I live..."

Religion   **Pages:232**

ISBN: *1-59462-160-8*   *MSRP* ***$17.95***

As a Man Thinketh
James Allen

"This little volume (the result of meditation and experience) is not intended as an exhaustive treatise on the much-written-upon subject of the power of thought. It is suggestive rather than explanatory, its object being to stimulate men and women to the discovery and perception of the truth that by virtue of the thoughts which they choose and encourage..."

Inspirational/Self Help   **Pages:80**

ISBN: *1-59462-231-0*   *MSRP* ***$9.45***

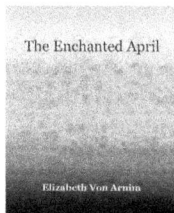

The Enchanted April
Elizabeth Von Arnim

It began in a woman's club in London on a February afternoon, an uncomfortable club, and a miserable afternoon when Mrs. Wilkins, who had come down from Hampstead to shop and had lunched at her club, took up The Times from the table in the smoking-room...

Fiction   **Pages:368**

ISBN: *1-59462-150-0*   *MSRP* ***$23.45***

Bringing Classics to Life

BOOK JUNGLE

www.bookjungle.com *email: sales@bookjungle.com fax: 630-214-0564 mail: Book Jungle PO Box 2226 Champaign, IL 61825*

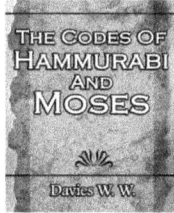

The Codes Of Hammurabi And Moses - W. W. Davies

The discovery of the Hammurabi Code is one of the greatest achievements of archaeology, and is of paramount interest, not only to the student of the Bible, but also to all those interested in ancient history...

Religion	Pages:132

ISBN: *1-59462-338-4*   *MSRP* **$12.95**

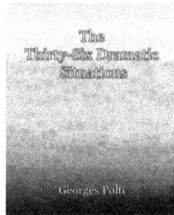

The Thirty-Six Dramatic Situations
Georges Polti

An incredibly useful guide for aspiring authors and playwrights. This volume categorizes every dramatic situation which could occur in a story and describes them in a list of 36 situations. A great aid to help inspire or formalize the creative writing process...

Self Help/Reference	Pages:204

ISBN: *1-59462-134-9*   *MSRP* **$15.95**

Holland - The History Of Netherlands
Thomas Colley Grattan

Thomas Grattan was a prestigious writer from Dublin who served as British Consul to the US. Among his works is an authoritative look at the history of Holland. A colorful and interesting look at history....

History/Politics	Pages:408

ISBN: *1-59462-137-3*   *MSRP* **$26.95**

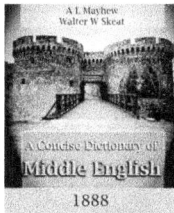

A Concise Dictionary of Middle English
A. L. Mayhew
Walter W. Skeat

The present work is intended to meet, in some measure, the requirements of those who wish to make some study of Middle-English, and who find a difficulty in obtaining such assistance as will enable them to find out the meanings and etymologies of the words most essential to their purpose...

Reference/History	Pages:332

ISBN: *1-59462-119-5*   *MSRP* **$29.95**

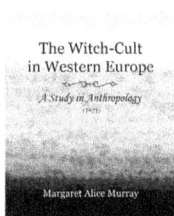

The Witch-Cult in Western Europe
Margaret Murray

QTY

The mass of existing material on this subject is so great that I have not attempted to make a survey of the whole of European "Witchcraft" but have confined myself to an intensive study of the cult in Great Britain. In order, however, to obtain a clearer understanding of the ritual and beliefs I have had recourse to French and Flemish sources...

Occult	Pages:308

ISBN: *1-59462-126-8*   *MSRP* **$22.45**

Bringing Classics to Life

BOOK JUNGLE

www.bookjungle.com *email: sales@bookjungle.com fax: 630-214-0564 mail: Book Jungle PO Box 2226 Champaign, IL 61825*

Name	
Email	
Telephone	
Address	
City, State ZIP	

☐ **Credit Card**   ☐ **Check / Money Order**

Credit Card Number	
Expiration Date	
Signature	

Please Mail to: Book Jungle
                PO Box 2226
                Champaign, IL 61825
or Fax to: 630-214-0564

ORDERING INFORMATION

web*: www.bookjungle.com*
email*: sales@bookjungle.com*
fax*: 630-214-0564*
mail*: Book Jungle PO Box 2226 Champaign, IL 61825*
or PayPal *to sales@bookjungle.com*

Please contact us for bulk discounts
DIRECT-ORDER TERMS

20% Discount if You Order
Two or More Books
Free Domestic Shipping!